NIGHTMARE IN BANGKOK

Andrew "Andy" Botts

ALOHA WAHOA WOMEN !.!
GREAT TO SEE YA
BACK AGAIN .!.!

MAHALO,

i/1/14

Poi Dog Publishers
HONOLULU, HAWAII

Dedicated to the women in my life:
My mother, wife, three sisters,
and editor, Laura Rectenwald

NIGHTMARE IN BANGKOK

Edited by Laura Rectenwald
First Edition

ISBN 978-1-60530-107-5

TABLE OF CONTENTS

CHAPTER ONE

BANGKOK - 1977

The Hawaiian gods blessed my journey with a fiery orange and red sunrise, silhouetting the lush green garden island of Kauai, as I flew west towards Bangkok on Pan Am flight 016. It was a vision that I saw, a vision of grandeur, as I contained the excitement burning within me with a breakfast Bloody Mary.

Thailand was under martial law in 1977, after the collapse of Saigon. It was the only noncommunist country left in Indochina. To avoid detection, we landed under the cover of pitch-black darkness. Instantly hit by a gush of hot air as I exited the airplane at midnight, it soon became an oily, sticky, and uncomfortable sweat from the humid Asian climate. I immediately focused on the Military Police in blue helmets holding M-16s. The atmosphere felt like I'd landed in the middle of the war zone. Atop the airport's sagging iron roof, burned-out neon lights barely lit up Bangkok International Airport. Once on the tarmac, I was crowded into a warm airport bus, and then shuttled to the main terminal.

I cringed when I entered Customs with a wad of hundred dollar bills in my wallet. Passengers from my flight were singled out, seemingly disappearing. In front of me, a team of MPs rummaged through a pair of duffle bags. The only language spoken was an

Asian dialect that I assumed was Thai, and I didn't speak a word if it. Fortunately, my clean-cut American profile didn't arouse suspicion, and I was cleared without delay. Not sure what to expect, I aimlessly wandered outside and was instantly swarmed by a throng of third-worlders. Amid the irritable chatter, "Taxi sir?" was the only English I could comprehend. Before I could say no, a seven-year-old boy with a crew cut and big grin snatched my suitcase from my hand and dragged it along the sidewalk until a taxi appeared. Meagerly I gave him a five-baht coin (25 cents). He gratefully clasped his hands together and bowed three times. For an extra buck, I probably could've bought his sister.

In the backseat of an old Toyota, air-conditioned by an oscillating fan positioned between the front and rear door, I expected to be driven to the city of Bangkok. A scrawny Asian with a flattop hairdo and bucked teeth, who looked as lost as I felt, sped down a vacant, dimly lit stretch of highway with fog lights. On the lookout for Commies, military checkpoints were set up like DUI stops every mile or so. After a short delay, we were waved through when they recognized that I was an American.

Craving a joint of pakalolo, I helplessly played charades with my non-English speaking driver, who responded, "Yes, yes," or "Girl?" to everything I said.

"No, not girl," I said, exasperated. "Elephant, Buddha, Thai weed.... You know, smoke, smoke."

"Smack?" he said, pointing to his arm with his index finger, mimicking a hypodermic needle.

"No, not smack. SMOKE, SMOKE!" I said, motioning towards my lips with my fingers, pantomiming a joint being smoked.

"Oh, ganja!" he finally figured out, the key word I was looking for.

"Yeah, ganja. Can you get?" I asked, elated.

"Yes, yes, ganja no ploblem. I get for you," he said, and then drove me to a rundown part of town that resembled a Chinatown of yesteryear. Up, down, around and through a maze of dark seedy backstreets, I thought that I was being set-up for a mug job when we arrived at a dimly lit hole-in-the-wall joint. Led out of my cab by the doorman, I expected to get rolled when the taxi disappeared with my suitcase in the trunk. Apprehensive, I held onto my wallet with a death grip as I looked over my shoulders. Urged into a back alley dog and pony show, my jaw dropped when I got inside. Fifteen gorgeous babes with silky smooth skin strutted naked onstage like cabaret dancers, legs flailing in unison. I gripped my wallet tighter.

Momma-san, the pimp of the house, aggressively promoted the playmate of my choice. Making me feel like I was gay if I didn't opt from her flock, I selected an older woman to be my girlfriend for the night. She was twenty-one years old, to my post-puberty age of twenty. Miraculously, my driver reappeared with a large bag of ganja and checked us into a sleazy hotel for the night.

Musty smelling, with a semi-cold air-conditioner that hummed like a B-52 bomber, the interior looked like it had been decorated by the Salvation Army. For $35.00, including the taxi, ganja and my girlfriend, it was a bargain to me. When I met Uncle Sam the following morning, he laughed when I told him how much I'd spent.

Uncle Sam was a short, thin, older Thai with glasses. He was my connection. Uncle Sam was a nickname he picked up from

American GI's during the Vietnam War. It was a Godsend to meet someone with a grasp of the English language. While in Bangkok, he introduced me to the typical Bangkok tourist scene —nightlife of live sex acts and ping-pong stunts that upstaged the Ringling Brothers Circus. To solidify our partnership, he took me to Pattaya Beach.

Pattaya Beach is a brightly colored neon lit strip of go-go bars and nightclubs. Chinese junks anchored in the calm harbor contrasted the horde of street vendors selling American cigarettes, blue jeans, leather belts and a variety of name brand goods. "Black Magic Woman" blared from an open-air bar, while a herd of taxi drivers circled the mile long strip. As if I was the only guy in Waikiki on New Years Eve, voluptuous Thai women swarmed me like dogs in heat. The Thai way of finding a husband—twelve bucks, bring her back tomorrow, fifty, bring her back next week. After a plethora of potential housewives, we continued north to Chiang Mai, an ancient Thai city near "The Golden Triangle."

Chiang Mai is on the outskirts of the triangular border of Burma, Laos and Thailand, where eighty percent of the world's heroin was manufactured. Considering that I looked more out of place than I felt, catching the late night bus was less conspicuous than a domestic flight. Boarding an old rusted bus, piss drunk, we found a pair of worn seats patched with green tape in the rear, near the restroom that reeked of urine. Amongst a degenerate bunch of misfits, all in dire need of major dental work, they pointed, smiled, and stared at me like a had shit on my face.

Over five hundred miles from Bangkok, the bus driver barreled down an endless two-lane stretch of jungle road in pitch-black darkness. Wide-awake for the grueling seven-hour ride, I wondered if I had gotten in over my head this time. An hour out of Chiang Mai, I caught my first glimpse of a land that time had forgotten. A brilliant orange sunrise shone through a forest of rubber trees, papaya groves and banana patches that hung over the highway. Palm thatched huts were tucked beneath the trees. Pigs and chickens wandered freely.

At the Chiang Mai bus depot, the mob of peasants unloaded bamboo baskets full of fruit and other produce from the bus. Uncle Sam quickly led me through the crowd. A cluster of tuk-tuks (flashy blue and yellow, two-seat, three-wheeled taxis) sat parked on the roadside. Uncle Sam spoke in Thai to the driver of a tuk-tuk. The driver babbled back while nodding his head. After squeezing into the tuk-tuk, we were taken to the Chiang Mai Inn.

The Chiang Mai Inn was a two-story structure made from Teak wood. Elaborate hand carved furniture adorned the interior. For $5.00 a night, I checked into a two-bed corner suite on the second floor. Surrounded by a forest of bamboo and ginger, it was cool and quiet compared to the sweltering madness of Bangkok. The fragrance and crisp air reminded me of a mountaintop cabin in Hawaii. On a mission to purchase a half-pound of China White heroin, known as CW, Uncle Sam explained the plan to me.

"Andrew, I need money. I go see my organization. No worly, maybe three days, mai pan rai (no problem). This is my life, top secret, no speak anything or GKKK," he said, as he mimicked a knife cutting his throat. After coming this far I had no choice but to trust him. Forking over $2000, half payment for eight ounces of heroin, including packaging, he parted.

Stranded, I went downstairs to the lobby of the inn. A small tour desk adorned the red and blue oriental-carpeted lobby. A coffee shop filled the rear. Various tours were available. Elephant rides and riverboat tours appeared to be the main attractions. A classy Thai lady with a friendly smile was very helpful without being pushy. While browsing through a brochure, I strolled into the coffee shop for lunch. An attractive Thai girl, with a smile that accentuated her high cheekbones, promptly sat me in a corner booth. "Somesing drink?" she asked with a wide smile.

"Yes, Singha beer, please," I said, and returned a smile.

Back in a snap, she had an ice-cold beer and a menu. "Where you from? What your name?" she asked, still smiling.

"My name is Andy. I'm from Hawaii," I said.

"Ha-why, where Ha-why?" she asked.

"America," I said simply, when I realized that she was out of touch with the world.

"Oh, USA, you so lucky," she said, "My name Tuk (Took)."

Another Thai girl approached my table with an order pad. Tuk introduced her to me as my waitress. While conversing in Thai, Tuk looked at me and giggled. "What'd she say?" I asked the waitress.

"She say, she want take you home," she said.

"Great! Let's go," I said, and made my move. I showed Tuk the brochures and hinted that I needed her as an interpreter and tour guide. Without hesitation, she volunteered to be my guide, and promptly changed her clothes while I scarfed down a plate of shrimp fried rice. After booking an elephant tour for the following day, we went back to my room where she offered to give me a massage.

Incredibly strong for such a petite girl, she, along with every other Thai girl, mastered the art of Asian massage. Painful, yet relieving, she cracked my neck, back, knuckles and toes. Turned onto my left side, she folded my arms across my chest. Pulling my left arm towards her, she jammed the right side of my butt with her foot. Twisted like a pretzel, every kink in my body cracked simultaneously. It became sensual when she worked her way down my butt and legs. I grabbed her slim waist and flipped her down next to me. "My turn," I said with a smile as I kissed her lips. Stripped down to her panties, I gave her an American massage—a backrub. I was in love and she was in love, puppy love, and we stayed in bed for the rest of the afternoon.

Holding hands, we toured the primitive city that evening. Besieged with vendors selling clothes and cheap souvenirs, amidst the hawkers, food stands displayed spicy Thai dishes. Tuk ordered a few Thai delicacies that looked gross and smelled worse. For me, the only safe dish seemed to be chicken cooked on an open barbecue. Chopped on a cutting board and packed into a plastic bag, a tiny bag of red sweet and sour Thai chili sauce was swiftly attached with a rubber band.

After dinner, I bought a few "Singha Beer" T-shirts as souvenirs. Everything was negotiable. For one dollar a pair, extravagant by Tuk's standards, I splurged and bought her five Pierre Cardin silk panties. Delighted by my generosity, she spent the rest of the evening modeling for me.

Energized by the thought of adventure, I awoke early the next morning for our expedition into the jungle. Sporting an Aloha shirt, Hang Ten shorts and rubber slippers, I felt right at home.

Tuk wore a tight white T-shirt, which displayed SINGHA BEER across her plump breasts, and red hot pants that revealed her genetically hairless legs. Towels in arm, we met our taxi guide in the lobby, who resembled every other taxi driver. Tuk conversed in Thai as he drove. I sat back and enjoyed the scenery.

Deep inside the rainforest, we got out and watched a small herd of elephants take their morning bath. Ten large elephants and two cute babies played in a wide shallow river. Sucking water into their trunks and shooting it out with the force of a fire hose, they mischievously sprayed each other in a water fight. Well-trained and obedient, they responded to a few taps with a thin bamboo stick, and immediately trekked out of the stream. What appeared to be their daily chore, they picked up large logs with their trunks, and neatly assembled a large pile within minutes. Like huge dogs, they faithfully obeyed orders of "Stop, go, kneel and roll over." On command, our elephant crouched down on its elbows so we could climb aboard. Planting my legs behind its ears, Tuk squeezed behind me with her arms tightly wrapped around my waist. Tromping off into the forest, with our guide in tow, we rode with the herd to the Mekok Waterfall.

A rainbow mist shrouded the thirty-foot high waterfall, as a river of rainwater cascaded over a shallow cave, splashing into a large, clear, ice-cold pond. Shamelessly taking off her hot pants, Tuk followed me into the icy water in her lavender panties and white T-shirt. I was enthralled by the wet T-shirt look. She didn't give it a second thought. The cave behind the waterfall was large enough for both of us. Once inside, our body heat kept us warm. After an hour of bliss, our guide arranged lunch.

A vendor in a makeshift stand sold food and beer. Basking in the warm sun on large round smooth rocks, we ate chicken and drank Singha beer while listening to the birds and waterfall. A tranquil world, Utopia, it was a place in time that I didn't want to leave. After a few hours, the herd of elephants had to return. Our tour then continued on to Doi Suthep temple, a renowned Buddhist temple thousands of feet above the city.

As we traversed the curvy mountainous road that led to the temple, it reminded me of the Beatles song, "The Long and Winding Road." Several miles later, we reached the base of the temple. The air was noticeably cooler, and the majestic view of the countryside was phenomenal. After climbing a hundred steep cement steps that must've taken a multitude of slaves to construct, we reached Doi Suthep temple.

The twelfth century temple displayed rare murals throughout the perimeter of the interior's ceiling. Near the border wall that surrounded the temple, a young Thai girl sold sparrows imprisoned in small bamboo cages. I bought a pair for five-baht (25 cents) and set them free. A spirit of compassion came over me, as they elatedly flapped their wings off into oblivion. At the top of the world looking down on creation, my guide told me where I really was.

"Opium grow here," he said, pointing to the mountains above and around us. "Hmong, Meo, Karen tribe live mountains, too much opium. Opium no ploblem, police cannot catch. Heloin, police catch, desa molee (you're dead)," he explained. Opium was legal until refined into heroin, twenty times stronger. Despite the severe penalties for heroin trafficking, drug busts were in the news daily. Martial law declared immediate trials. Arrested today, convicted tomorrow, executed at sunrise the following morning.

Gazing at the vast mountain range, I could only imagine the magnitude of opium poppies being grown. "Can I see?" I asked curiously.

"You want smoke opium?" he asked.

"No smoke, only see," I said cautiously, remembering Uncle Sam's warning of keeping quiet. I also learned that taxi drivers were famous for selling drugs to foreigners and then turning them in for a reward. "Only want to see flowers, take picture," I said with a smile, holding my camera up.

"Yes, yes, no ploblem. Tomollow I see you hotel. Tomollow moaning, eight o-cock," he said eagerly, pointing to his watch.

Awoken to the sound of roosters, my adrenaline was pumping with excitement. Tuk stayed in bed for the day. I met my guide in the lobby. Instead of taking me to the opium fields, he took me to a Thai silk factory. I wanted to slap him for the detour, but had to go along with his game. Apparently, taxi drivers got kickbacks for taking customers to factories.

In a small, barn-like building set around a gravel driveway and large open field, three large encased bins exhibited the evolving stages of silk worms. The first bin simulated something out of a science fiction movie. Adorned with fresh green leaves, large green caterpillars slinked around in a massive orgy. The next bin had an excess of yellow striped worms in the silk cocoon stage of their lives. The last bin had a multitude of beautifully colored butterflies fluttering about, mating and continuing the cycle.

Led into the factory, I noticed a variety of colorful silk ties near the door. Huge rolls of Thai silk hung from the walls. I was immediately given a free beer served on a shiny brass platter with oriental carvings. Feeling obligated, I bought a few silk ties. Downing my beer, which was re-filled twice, I was anxious to see the poppy fields.

Driven back up the long and winding road to Doi Suthep temple, my guide detoured onto a dirt road a mile past the temple. After a short drive in, a long row of makeshift, palm-thatched huts displayed items sold by women from the Karen hill tribe. Dressed in long black pajama type costumes, decorated with colored beads and macramé, the Indian faced women sold a variety of handmade opium pipes, silver necklaces and other primitive souvenirs.

For the next leg of my journey, my guide arranged transportation with a Thai boy on a motorcycle. He packed me into the jungle on the back of his beat-up Yamaha dirt bike. My guide faithfully waited behind. Holding on for dear life, he gunned it down the flood-rutted jungle trail that served as a road. Weaving in and out of trees, we eventually reached a village of bamboo huts with palm-thatched roofs. Chickens, pigs, and naked children roamed tamely and freely. From children to adults, everyone wore the black tribal costumes. Two older tribesmen with sucked up prune faces approached us.

"Smoke opium?" they asked me.

"No, take picture," I said with a smile, showing them my camera. My biker babbled something in Thai.

"Cup, mai me pen ha," the tribesman replied, which I took to mean yes, and then followed them on foot into the jungle. We trekked down a narrow trail through a forest of plants similar to those in Hawaii. Seemingly on a journey to no-man's land, after an hour's hike through the jungle, we came to a clearing. Several bamboo huts were spread along the landscape, surrounded by fields of poppies. Hundreds of women dressed in black tribal costumes waded into the chest-high fields of red and white tulip-like flowers. With a sharp tool that resembled an old can opener, they tirelessly whipped through the fields at marathon speed, making incisions around the sides of the green bulbs. White sap oozed from the bulbs. It hardens overnight. The bulbs are scraped the following day. Large wicker baskets were filled to the brim with balls of opium. A few addict supervisors nodded under the shade of a hut.

"Smoke opium?" I was asked again.

I had smoked heroin once before, but it made me nauseous and sick. My only interest was in the enormous profits. Opium was harmless in comparison, and seemed to be the thing to do after coming this far. Smiling and nodding my head willingly, I visited my first opium den in the middle of the Golden Triangle.

I followed them into a hut. Weaved palm leaf mats surrounded a small fire that burned on the clay floor. The tribesman packed a bamboo pipe full of the tarry substance. Lying on my side with my head on a small, hard, matted pillow, I held the pipe upside down with a candle underneath. After exhaling deeply, I sucked the sour tasting smoke into my lungs, and held my breath for thirty seconds. When I released the smoke, I felt a soothing, mellow, euphoric high lift my head and give my body a content feeling. After four more bowls, I was in another world.

"Heloin?" he whispered, showing me a vile of white powder.

"No thanks," I said with a smile. I wasn't going all the way.

The sun was setting by the time we hiked out and I was biked back to the main road. Worn out and still high, my taxi-guide awaited my return, and then took me back to the Chiang Mai Inn. Tuk cheerfully greeted me when I returned, and massaged me until I passed out.

On the third day, Uncle Sam returned with eight ounces of China White heroin. Concealed into the bottom of a new briefcase, the workmanship was flawless. Uncle Sam then coached me on the questioning tactics used by Customs agents to detect mules. He told me that I'd be asked an assortment of questions and then emphasized that my reaction was imperative. Prepared for my return to Honolulu, I was ready for my flight from Chiang Mai the following morning. Uncle Sam caught the bus back to Bangkok. I spent my last night with Tuk. Sadly, I said goodbye the following morning, and never saw her again.

Although the heroin was expertly packaged, I couldn't help being apprehensive when I entered the small domestic airport at Chiang Mai. After being frisked at the entrance, my suitcase and briefcase were thoroughly checked and X-rayed. Military Police holding M-16s stood out at every corner. They seemed to be scrutinizing me. My only hope was to avoid eye contact and smile perpetually. No longer among a crowd of peasants, from my observations the Thais had just two social classes—the extremely rich and the exceedingly poor. No middle class. Older military officials with serious faces strutted around with an aura of supremacy. They seemed to be running the country. I continued smiling. Several paranoid hours later, I boarded my Thai Airways flight to Bangkok, and connected with my flight to Honolulu. My nerves eased when my Pan Am flight lifted off the runway.

When I arrived in Hawaii, I casually walked up to the inspection counter. Ready for my con routine, I laid my suitcase, garment bag and heroin-lined briefcase in front of the inspector. After a brief computer check, the inspector pushed a black button to the left of his computer. A tall, middle-aged agent, who had been casing everyone, immediately walked over. He went directly to the briefcase. "All right, pull out the bottom," he demanded.

My heart dropped. I thought he had been tipped off, but I had to maintain my composure. "What do you mean pull out the bottom?" I chuckled, "The bottom doesn't come out."

He wasn't fooled by my casual response. "Where did you go?" he asked, while pushing and prodding the bottom of the briefcase.

"Bangkok," I replied.

"What was the purpose of going to Bangkok?" "How long did you stay?" "Where else did you go?" "Why Bangkok?" he asked rapid fire.

"Pleasure." "Fourteen days." "No where else." "I'm going to college in California. My parents bought me a trip to the Orient. I didn't have time to go anywhere else." I lied in succession to his questions.

He picked up the briefcase and looked at it from different angles. "Where'd you buy this briefcase?" he asked.

"I bought it in Marina Del Ray."

"Where in Marina Del Ray?" he asked quickly.

"I don't know, some small store outside of the shopping center," I said.

He twirled it around in his hands and examined the sides. "Where's the manufacturer's label?" he asked. "Everything sold in the U.S. has to have a manufacturer's label. This has no manufacturer's label. Are you sure that you didn't buy this in Hong Kong or somewhere?"

He had me, but I couldn't change my story. "I'm positive where I bought it," I maintained. He picked up the briefcase and took it through a closed door. My heart sunk to my feet. *I pushed my luck this time*, I thought. I had visions of being arrested and taken to Halawa Jail.

He returned ten minutes later and put the briefcase on the counter. "O.K., good enough," he said. "Clear him."

"Good enough?" I said. "Oh, good enough," I repeated, stunned. I quickly gathered my stuff, and got out of there before he changed his mind.

When I tore apart the briefcase, I found the CW factory-pressed between two thin slices of balsa wood. A hard, flat, heroin sandwiched board an eighth of an inch thick lay snug beneath the felt lining. Four ounces of white powder was spread inside the bottom, and four ounces on top. Wholesale price, uncut, was $10,000 an ounce. My connections with the Hawaiian mob now looked to me as their connection. The following year I made another run and recruited a high school friend as a mule.

I sent my mule on a tour through Japan and Hong Kong. We met in Bangkok afterwards. This time we used a briefcase with

American manufacturer's labels. Uncle Sam went to Chiang Mai. I stayed in Bangkok.

I became a tourist victim. Every time that I caught a taxi, I was taken to a temple, massage parlor or jewelry store, including a three-story gem factory. A robber's smash and grab dream, a massive inventory of jade, sapphires and rubies were displayed in glass cases. For $200, I bought an emerald green "Imperial jade" stone. For an extra fifty bucks, it was set in an 18-karat gold ring to my specifications. Fascinated with the diversity of gems, I learned a legitimate trade that I could've pursued. The dangerous life had a different glamour though.

Within a week my mule arrived, and Uncle Sam returned from Chiang Mai with the heroin-lined briefcase. Upon our return to Hawaii, U.S. Custom's agents immediately escorted me to secondary. In route, my mule walked out the front door, briefcase in hand.

To keep a low profile, I resided in San Francisco from 1977–1979, and unloaded my merchandise in Hawaii. Confident of their expertise in packaging, the next few loads were mailed to me in felt-lined silverware sets, sent under my girlfriend's name, through San Francisco. Like a spoiled rich kid, I wined and dined at the finest restaurants, and splurged on new cars, clothes and jewelry.

CHAPTER TWO

THE GAME

The 1975 Duke Kahanamoku surf meet was on, the surf was huge, and Kamehameha highway was jam-packed. Beachside parking was crammed with rental vehicles as I pulled into Sunset Beach in a Datsun 1200. Within seconds, Mike popped open the trunk of a Toyota and absconded with an armload of purses, wallets and cameras.

Mike looked like a criminal, with his tattoos, missing teeth, and wild black hair. The Game was a daily routine of driving around Hawaii on an endless vacation, all expenses paid, and picking the locks of vehicles marked with rental agency stickers. The game was also called "banging cars." I was a teenager serving as Mike's get-away driver and protégé banger.

I pulled back onto Kamehameha highway and headed towards Kailua. I kept my eye in the rear view mirror. Mike began searching the pile of goods on the passenger's floor. I immediately noticed a black LTD behind us. "Hold it Mike. Vice," I said, "Don't look back. Sit up." They followed us for a hundred yards. My heart sank when the small blue lights in the grill started flashing. "Oh no. They're pulling us over," I said.

"Split, split," Mike yelled frantically as I pulled off the road, "Split, split! What the f... you doing?"

"Shut up. Look forward. Wait," I spat back. I needed time to figure out a plan.

Two gorillas got out of the LTD and casually strolled towards us. Mike was having a fit. "Split, split!" he continued, "Get the hell out of here. What the f... you doing? You crazy or what?"

I had a hunch that it was a fluke stop, because they would've pounced on us if we were staked-out. First gear engaged, my foot on the clutch pedal, I waited until they got to the rear of my car. Flooring it, I popped the clutch, pulled a 180-degree fishtail, and headed back to Sunset Beach. I could see their surprised faces as I spun past. They ran back to their LTD.

I forgot about the Duke meet and the jam-packed road. There was no way through the traffic without a casualty. While doing a peripheral scan of Sunset Beach with one eye, I watched the LTD in my mirror. I gained a hundred yards on them. A gravel road ran parallel to the highway, hidden behind the hale koa brush. At the end of the brush was the entrance.

"Get ready Mike," I said. "When I say 'go', throw everything out the window." My foot remained imbedded on the gas pedal. Winding out in third gear, I grinded gears downshifting into second. I hit the gravel road and counter-steered completely to the left. We did a perfect four-wheel drift around the brush. "Now Mike, GO!" I shouted, once I lost complete view of the cops. The evidence landed deep into the brush, and the chase began.

Full throttle, five cops in tow, sirens blaring, I passed on the left and on the sugar cane road to my right. From Sunset Beach to Kahuku, I gave them a high-speed chase for seven miles. A hundred yards away, a dragnet of children held out red stop signs. Kahuku School had just gotten out. The end of the line, getting through wasn't an option.

"Quick, let me out," Mike begged as we approached Kahuku Hospital.

Slamming on the brakes, I screeched to a halt. Mike jumped out and ran up the gravel road. I tried to pull back onto the highway. I got about thirty feet before a squad of angry cops forced me over. Before I could open my door, two raging bulls pulled me out through the window by my long sun-bleached hair.

"What the f... you doing?" they shouted in-between rib-shots, as they dragged me across the gravel. "Why were you running? Who was your friend?" they demanded, as they threw me in and out of a hedge.

"I don't know the guy. He was a hitchhiker. He made me run," I said, in-between short breaths.

"You're under arrest," they said as they handcuffed me. "Careless driving."

The squad then went off in search of Mike. I was left at the scene with a fat Japanese sergeant. He had a crew cut, a pig snout nose, and was visibly pissed. "What punk, you think its funny?" he asked, as I sat on the front passenger's seat of my car, handcuffed behind my back.

"No," I said quietly, avoiding eye contact.

Bending down to eye level, he swung his right fist toward my ribcage. Spontaneously, I twisted my body to the left. My right arm blocked his punch. He became enraged. Determined to break my ribs, he got in closer and swung harder. Turning left again, my right arm caught his punch once more. His face contorted with anger. I could hear the angry snorts protruding from his snout. Squeezing the top half of his body into my car, he pinned my right shoulder to the seat with his left hand, and wound up with his right fist.

I should've been worried and scared, but I wasn't. In my heart I refused to believe what was happening. I knew that I was wrong and deserved punishment, but for a cop to break my ribs while handcuffed behind my back was worse. I couldn't accept wrong for wrong.

He had an open shot of my ribs and swung with all of his might. Right before impact, his fist connected with the sharp edge of the hard, plastic-edged glove box that was left open, breaking it off its hinges in a snap. I immediately noticed the four skin-scraped round caps of blood where his knuckles used to be. I wanted to laugh, but knew better. Sucking wind through his teeth in pain, his eyes rolled as he grabbed a handkerchief from his pocket and wrapped his hand up.

Was that the power of believing without a doubt, or do I have a Guardian Angel with miraculous powers? I asked myself, and continue to ask.

They found Mike hiding in a car at Kahuku high school. We were both arrested and taken to the Wahiawa police station on the North Shore. They still didn't know about the theft, so Mike was released without charges. I posted $50.00 bail for the careless driving charge. Under the guise of a massive sick-in, dubbed the "Blue flu," the entire Honolulu police force went on strike on the day of my trial (cops are prohibited from striking in Hawaii). Without the cop's testimony, the careless driving charge was dismissed.

Inherently, my adventurous nature ran in the blood. Born in Honolulu, in the pre-statehood year of 1956, I was named after my great-grandfather, Andrew Jackson Botts, who joined the Civil War when he was twelve and a half years old. Known as "The Little Drummer Boy," he was decorated as the youngest soldier at the end of the Civil War, North and South.

Like father, like son—my grandfather, E.J. Botts, left home when he was fourteen years old, and found his way to the Territory of Hawaii in 1913. E.J. was a well-revered criminal attorney for over fifty years, and held a number of high-level government positions, including 'U.S. Commissioner for the District of Hawaii' from 1920–1929.

Old Hawaii was a close knit, "who you know" community. Reputations and class dictated your status. Charlie Chan was based on a real life Honolulu Detective, who my grandfather knew well, along with anyone else of importance. E.J. was a fix-it lawyer. He had the connections. "The old Godfather of Honolulu," among other stories that filtered through over the years, remembered best was when he tried a woman for prostitution.

The prostitute's defense rested on her reputable status. "Name just one household, just one respectable member of this community that you know," E.J. asked her.

"Your own," she said, "I know Dickie Botts."

The talk of the town, Richard "Dickie" Botts was my father. Born in Honolulu in 1917, he was the eldest of three children. A lively and colorful character in Honolulu, Dickie was a Waikiki beachboy, womanizer and alcoholic. Unfortunately, alcohol was his downfall, which led to a bitter divorce when I was eight years old. He eventually died of kidney failure.

My three sisters and I were raised by my mother, Jackie. Jackie was a mom that everybody loved, and loved most of my friends in return. At the same time, she didn't put up with any B.S., and wouldn't hesitate to release an occasional backhand. An optimist, she instilled a firm belief that everything in life happens for a reason, and the worst always happens for the best. A belief crucial to survive in this insane world, I digested this principle when I was young.

I grew up in Kailua, on the countryside of the island of Oahu. Kailua High School was "The highest school in the State of Hawaii." The administration implemented a three-year pilot-program in 1971, my sophomore year. It was a modular program designed after college schedules, with our class times staggered to give us ample study time. Most of us thought outside of the box. It was idle time to get high and find escape routes from school. When the surf was up, the school was empty. The only things that I learned were how to roll a joint, score dope and spot a Nark. Kailua was a party town. Known as "The Botts parties," I threw the biggest parties in Kailua. In step with the party life, I completed a bartender's training course when I turned eighteen —the legal drinking age then.

Life was a game. Everything I did was a game. I had a scofflaw attitude and accumulated traffic tickets faster than I could disregard them. Under the traffic system of the seventies, if you failed to appear in court after being cited, a Penal Summons would be issued. This meant that the cops would have to find you, have you sign the summons, and set a new court date. If you didn't go to court on the new date, then a bench warrant would be issued and you'd be arrested for contempt of court.

I couldn't imagine why anybody would even consider going to court the first time around. Swiftly throwing away all tickets, I continued speeding, running red lights, and disregarding "no parking" signs. A few years and over a hundred tickets later, it caught up to me when I tried to renew my driver's license. Like a part-time job, I went to court three times a week, with six tickets at a time, for over six months. Inspired by the court drama, I fought every citation, and won most of them due to various legal technicalities. This served as on-the-job Law School, and fueled my teenage delinquency. It was another game, the game of getting away with it.

Banging cars was lucrative, exciting and addicting. There was a thrill to scoring fast cash and getting away with crime. Using a slim screwdriver, I mastered the various angles, turns, and jiggles of most car doors and trunks. Faster than Houdini, I became the Yogi Bear of bangers. The only penalty was being held in the police station for up to forty-eight hours pending an investigation. After forty-eight hours we were released without charges, by law, as the state couldn't afford to bring tourists back to Hawaii for a trial, which was essential to get a conviction.

The rules for the cops were to catch us and beat the crap out of us. To sting a banger, the only way they could get a conviction was by using a set-up vehicle. A set-up vehicle was a car that the cops rented and parked in a high profile theft area. They would place a purse or wallet containing over $200 inside of the car, the amount necessary to convict for a felony, and then stake out the set-up vehicle until a banger grabbed the bait.

The Alpha squad was a theft-robbery unit assigned to the town side of Oahu, while the vice-squad watched the country part of the island. Known as "Town and Country," the Koolau mountain range separated Honolulu, the town side, from the country part of the island. Chased by foot, car or helicopter, the Alpha squad pursued me daily with a passion. My invincibility frustrated them intensely, as I outwitted them on stakeouts and set-ups constantly. I thought that I was invincible, and they must've thought so too. At the top of the Honolulu Police Department's most wanted list, it got to the point where I couldn't go anywhere, anytime, without being followed or pulled over.

"Whenever I go to church and they talk about the devil, I think of you," a cop told me. He wanted to hang me from the Pali Lookout, to "Kill the devil."

The Pali Lookout is at the top of the Koolau mountain range, two thousand feet above sea level. Pali means cliff in Hawaiian. Legend has it that King Kamehameha conquered the islands by throwing the warriors over the Pali. The Pali was my favorite spot. It was also the hottest place for stakeouts. Surrounded by Pine trees and wild ginger, it has a crisp, sweet aroma in the air. The scenic point is a short walk from the parking lot, and has a view that kept the tourists mesmerized while I ripped them off. I spotted the Alpha squad watching me with binoculars one day, so I knew where they hid.

On another occasion, I had a strong feeling that it was staked out. To confirm my instincts, I sent Gus up into the mountains. Gus was a dedicated criminal who had more guts than brains. "Lie all the way and never confess," was his motto, which is why I trusted him. The Alpha squads spotted Gus first, so they played hide and seek with him. Gus couldn't find them. I was certain that they were there, but ignored my instincts. In a matter of seconds, I popped open the trunks of several cars in a row.

Before I knew it, ten unmarked cars flew into the parking lot Hawaii 5-0 style, fishtailing around corners and climbing curbs. I was petrified when they jumped out of their cars and rushed us. Vernon, a large Hawaiian cop with a personal vengeance, grabbed me by the hair. "Botts is mine!" he demanded.

The rest of the squad grabbed Gus. "You looking for us?" they said cheerfully as they slapped his head, "Here we are." Gus was shoved around roughly and taken into the forest so nobody could witness the brutality. Expecting the worst, Vernon took me off to the side. Surprisingly, he sat me down on the curb between two cars.

"You know what, I've gotta take my hat off to you," he said admirably. "Of all these guys playing the game, you're the fastest and the best. I timed you opening a trunk one time and it took you two seconds," he emphasized with two fingers extended.

"Oh, I guess I had trouble with that lock," I said, when I realized that he wasn't going to beat me.

"If I wasn't a cop, I'd hire you to work for me. How do you do it?" he asked baffled. "I'm here all day freezing my ass off waiting for you, and half the time you don't show up. But when you do show up, you know we're here. Yet of all the times we've pulled you over, you've never had a scanner (police radio). How do you do it?"

"I don't know, I guess I've got a good sixth sense," I said, and shrugged my shoulders. At the time, I didn't understand it either. All I knew was that I could sense cops and money, a distinct feeling of fear or excitement, which I probably noticed because they were very important to me. I call it the "God within," the intuitive side known as our instincts. It's the spiritual part of us that's hard to recognize, understand and trust.

"Well I'm tired of arresting you," he said, exasperated, "because you always walk even when we do catch you. The next time I'm just going to shoot you," he said, dead serious. The squad then returned with Gus, beaten to a pulp, and formally arrested us. Released pending an investigation the following day, once again, it became routine.

I drove around the island from sunrise to sunset everyday. Always on my guard, I habitually drove with one eye in the rear view mirror and the other on the road. I didn't have to push my luck. The scores would either be there or they weren't. Similar to playing in a casino, I believed in omens and lucky streaks. I never chased a bad streak, which was the case at Hanauma Bay one day.

Hanauma Bay is a popular beach and scenic point. Over two hundred cars park there on any given day. Beachgoers usually locked their valuables in the trunks, where it was "safe." At Hanauma Bay, I didn't open the doors—I opened the trunks. In a matter of seconds, I popped the trunks of ten cars in a row. Every trunk was empty. I took it as a bad streak and quit for the day.

When I drove out of the parking lot, a squad of cop cars swarmed down the only entrance/exit. I automatically tossed my screwdriver out the window. It turned out that one of the cars that I banged was a set-up vehicle. A wallet had been placed under the passenger's seat with $250 in cash. They missed their sting. Since I jimmied the lock, I was arrested for criminal property damage. Like my traffic tickets, I took the case to trial.

In court, three officers testified that they watched me go down the line of cars with my back to them. "With a foreign object," they saw me open all of the cars in a matter of seconds. Since the screwdriver wasn't recovered, my lawyer argued that I could've had a pass key. The judge agreed and the case was dismissed.

I did have a personal vow to stop. "If they can convict me for a felony, I'll hang up my screwdriver," I said. I got my wish when they pinned me for a guitar that I hadn't stolen. I fought the case and lost, although I should've won. Considering all that I had gotten away with, I accepted it as karma, and hung up my screwdriver. At twenty years old, I'd had my fun, and sincerely planned to go straight. While awaiting sentencing, I enrolled in a restaurant management school in California.

Four weeks before sentencing, I drove over the Pali in a beat-up 1967 Volkswagen Van. I was flat broke. A strong urge that felt like a spiritual driving force was urging me into the Pali Lookout. I had to resist this urge. It'd sabotage my sentencing if I got busted. As I got closer to the lookout, the urge got stronger. Like an addictive crave, I couldn't control it. *Just looking won't hurt,* soon became, *C'mon God, give me one last big one and I'll never do it again. I'll go straight, everything.*

As I pulled into the parking lot, an older Asian couple with gold teeth and flower leis walked away from a Cadillac with their chauffer. She didn't have her purse in hand. They simultaneously disappeared from view as I parked to the right of the Caddie. A Gucci purse sat on the backseat. In and out of the car in seconds, I re-locked it to leave the disappeared into thin air effect.

A surge of excitement pumped my heart as I drove towards Kailua. I could feel the wealth in the purse. I anxiously pulled onto an old back road that led to Maunawili and searched it. Inside, I found a thick stack of crisp hundred dollar bills, and a large pouch filled with jewelry.

When I got home, I counted the loot and examined the stones. I thought that the diamond encrusted, five-karat emerald ring, set in 18kt white gold, was green plastic surrounded by rhinestones. *Nobody sets diamonds in silver*, I thought, not knowing that it was white gold. Diamonds, emeralds and rubies were discarded into my trashcan without a second thought. It was all costume jewelry as far as I knew. Fringes compared to the cash, I kept the jade, pearls, fiery opals and thick eighteen-karat gold chains. I learned the truth the following morning when I read the front page of the *Honolulu Advertiser*. "Over $35,000 in cash and jewelry," I quickly dove back into my trashcan and recovered the real gems.

Four weeks later, I appeared in court for sentencing. My arrest record was extensive, but I had no felony convictions. I showed the court my college acceptance letter, and promised to leave the state. The prosecutor "stood mute." I was given a break and sentenced to a week in Halawa jail, followed by five years of probation. Probation meant nothing to me.

The old Halawa jail housed about one hundred and fifty pre-trial and short-term inmates. Short terms were a taste of reality, which was a deterrent to crime. Long-term sentences were imposed only when there was no chance of rehabilitation. The fear of a long term had a psychological impact. Eliminate the threat and it's no longer a deterrent. Long prison terms become a criminal bonding experience. They meet new connections, adapt to institutional life, and have time to plot out their next scam. It becomes their way of life. The prison population statewide was about five hundred in 1977, the same as it was in 1900, and up until then. Twenty years later it suddenly increased ten-fold.

The week seemed like eternity. I couldn't imagine bearing the boredom of the longer terms of six or twelve months. I was confined to a thirty by fifteen-foot holding tank with dark green bars, six bunk beds, a single toilet and a push button shower. Six holding tanks were aligned together with a TV posted outside of the bars, shared between two tanks.

I couldn't fathom going a day without a joint, much less a week, so I smuggled in four sticks of Thai weed sown into my slippers. As the only person in jail with pakalolo, I made a lot of friends (connections), including a Thai heroin smuggler whom I had read about in the newspapers. I was familiar with the incredible profits that heroin dealers made, which I learned from fencing stolen goods to the local drug dealers. Now I had a chance of connecting with the source of this valuable drug. To gain his confidence, I showed him a stick of Thai weed that I snuck into jail. Convinced that I was a smuggler, he arranged a meeting with his organization in Thailand. I thought that I hit the jackpot of rackets. My plans of staying straight and going to school instantly changed. I reneged on my promise to God. I had it all figured out, everything except the habit that I acquired from my product, and the withdrawals when I ran out.

Known as the jones, going through heroin withdrawals is a torturous fate of unrelenting physical and psychological torment. It includes constant vomiting, uncontrollable diarrhea, migraine headaches, insomnia, and continuous pain in every muscle and joint for up to a month. Death often seems to be a better option.

My connection escaped from McNeil Island Federal Penitentiary in 1979, and I lost contact with Uncle Sam. Without my steady, easy income, my stash of illegal gains dwindled. I returned to Hawaii from San Francisco. Heroin became my drug of choice and a habit I couldn't kick. Left with few alternatives, I banged cars again to feed my habit.

The cops were frustrated, especially the Alpha squad. Arrested once again, we reached a compromise. Under the condition that I leave the island by midnight, Lt. Anderson of the Alpha squad would release me without charges. With no intention of leaving, I agreed, and broke my promise without a second thought.

A few months later, I visited Kualoa Beach Park with Gus. Kualoa Beach Park is a quarter mile of beachfront, facing Chinaman's hat (a hat shaped island). A white gravel road runs parallel to an immense hedge of tall, thick hale koa trees, which separates the parking lot from the park's shoreline. Kualoa was under the jurisdiction of the country cops, not the Alpha squad, but their set-up tactics were similar.

A lone Toyota rental car was parked in the last parking lot. I pulled alongside the passenger's side, four-feet away, and aligned my driver's door with the Toyota's front passenger door. This created a perfect visual block from two angles, the right side, which faced the beach, and the front side once my driver's door was opened. Crouching below view level, I quickly opened the Toyota, snatched the black purse that was on the floor, and passed it to Gus.

"How much money?" I asked Gus, as I sped toward the only exit from the park.

"There's no wallet," Gus replied.

"What?" I asked, "What do you mean no wallet? Every purse has a wallet."

"No wallet, only traveler's checks," he said.

"Traveler's checks. How much?" I asked.

"There are five $50.00 checks. $250," Gus said.

"It's a set-up!" I realized. I knew that cops used traveler's checks in set-ups, and $250 would make the crime a felony. Cranking the steering wheel completely to the left, I punched the gas pedal and did a doughnut in the gravel. I returned to the Toyota, tossed the purse back inside, and then headed to the exit at a normal speed.

Halfway out of the park, a white van with two plainclothes cops sped towards us. Swerving to cut me off, in a near collision they blocked our path with the van. "Hold it! Police," the driver ordered with his gun and badge out.

"What seems to be the problem, officer?" I asked calmly, knowing that I had outsmarted them.

"Get out. Hands on the roof," he commanded. "What's your name?" he asked. He was ecstatic when I told him my name. I smiled when he rubbed his palms together gleefully.

"Where's the purse?" his partner demanded, after he searched my car.

"I'm thorry offither, but I don't carry a purth. But you can thee my wallet if you want," I said with a lisp.

They were stunned. His partner jumped in the van and sped back to the set-up vehicle. The purse was still inside. They arrested us anyway. Gus was released later that evening. I remained pending an investigation.

When Gus was released, five cops surrounded him. He thought that he was going to get beat-up again. Instead, they asked him if they could pray for him. I still wonder why they didn't pray for me.

The following morning I was charged with theft in the first degree—a felony. Bail was set at $10,000; ten times the standard amount. I took it as a tactic to quell my invincibility, and made bail within the hour.

A month later, the Alpha squad on a stakeout at Hanauma Bay arrested me. Unlike the Kualoa case, it wasn't a police set-up vehicle. It was a Japanese tourist from Osaka, Japan. I stole $298 from their trunk. I considered it an easy victory, a no-brainer. The state didn't bring tourists back for theft, especially Japan.

Ten minutes before the end of the forty-eight hour investigation, I anxiously stood by the cell door. Like music to my ears, I heard my name called. "Yeah, over here," I called out. "What? Released pending an investigation?" I asked expectedly.

"No you're being charged," the cellblock officer replied.

"What? Charged?" I said, surprised.

He took me out of my cell and led me to the receiving area. A detective greeted me there. I was formally charged with theft in the first degree. Bail was set at $20,000; twenty times the usual bail requirement.

"Twenty thousand dollars," I exclaimed, "Where am I going to get that kind of money? Shit, murder is less than that!"

"The prosecutor wants you off the streets. You made bail at ten thousand, so he's doubling it," the detective said with a smile.

As soon as he left, I turned to the cellblock officer. "Can I make my one phone call please?" I made bail again, and wished I could've seen their faces when they found out. The following morning, I appeared in District Court for an arraignment and plea.

Dressed in a deep-blue Yves Saint Laurent velvet suit, light blue silk shirt, thick eighteen-karat gold chain fashioned into a tie, two-karat diamond ring and diamond studded Rolex Presidential watch, all stolen, I flaunted it all into court. Peter Carlisle was my prosecutor. An East-coast haole who resembled Peter Sellers, Carlisle was the head of a Career Criminal unit.

Prior to my arraignment, Donna Woo met me in the hallway. Donna was the Public Defender who sent me down the road on my first felony conviction. She informed me that she'd be representing me again, and that Carlisle sought to have my bail revoked. Sleeping with the enemy was the way I saw it. I fired her on the spot.

"You can't do that. You know that you're just trying to buy time," she protested. She knew that I couldn't be sent to jail without an attorney, and knew that I knew it also.

"Call it what you want honey," I said, "but I'm entitled to a private attorney of my choice. You're fired." We then proceeded into court.

Upon entering my not-guilty plea, Prosecutor Carlisle immediately jumped up. "Your honor, we want to commit this man without bail," he demanded.

"Your honor, I want to fire my attorney," I shot back.

"What is this case?" asked the older Japanese judge presiding. He knew me from traffic court. The last time that I appeared before him he suspended my driver's license. It was the fifth time in six months that my license had been suspended. Traffic offenses were trivial in comparison though, so he was noticeably curious to hear what I had done this time.

"Theft, your honor," I said.

"And how much is the bail?" he asked, looking perplexed.

"Twenty thousand dollars," I said.

"Twenty thousand dollars!" he exclaimed. "And, and, you posted that much already, Mr. Botts?" he stuttered in disbelief.

"Yes, your honor," I said humbly, knowing that he was going to rule in my favor.

"I'm sorry Mr. Prosecutor. I refuse to touch this case," he said with his hands up. "If you want to commit this man without bail, I suggest you seek an indictment and take this matter to the Circuit Court. I refuse to touch it," he said firmly, and thumped his gavel on the desk.

Infuriated, Carlisle slammed his books together and stomped out of the courtroom. *Who's that haole think he's kidding? I* chuckled to myself, not realizing he'd one day be the uncontested City Prosecutor of Honolulu.

I could've hired the best attorney in Hawaii, a family friend, but knowing my past he suggested I enter a drug rehabilitation program. I couldn't fathom such a thing, so I hired Winston Mirikitani instead. Mirikitani was a crooked, but brilliant trial lawyer. "The White Knight," he always wore a white suit into court like he was auditioning for the Don Ho show. Now that I had a private attorney to manipulate the system, I could drag the case on for years if I had to.

CHAPTER THREE

OAHU PRISON (OP)

A month after my arraignment, Prosecutor Carlisle secured an indictment and filed a "Commitment without Bail" motion in Circuit Court. "Yeah, that's what he tried in District Court when I was arraigned," I informed Mirikitani. "What's this commitment without bail thing anyway?" I asked. "I've never heard of such a thing before."

"Oh it's nothing," he assured me casually. "They can't do that. It's unconstitutional. This isn't a capitol case, and you're not a flight risk."

"Yeah, but what's the chances of them getting away with it?" I asked warily. I knew the system well by then. Justice didn't matter in the lower courts. They did whatever they wanted. Legality was just another game.

"Don't worry, you've got a 90% chance of staying on the streets," he said confidently.

"Ninety percent! Is that all?" I asked.

Realizing his error, he quickly picked up the motion and scanned it again. "No, 99% you'll still be walking the streets."

Even with 99–1 odds in my favor, I knew otherwise. It was a familiar pattern; there are no odds. The hearing was in a week.

A week left of freedom was the way I saw it. I couldn't imagine going to jail without drugs, so I caught the midnight flight to Bangkok. Since I had lost contact with Uncle Sam, I had to wing it. Using the oldest trick in the book, I bought a fake tennis ball can from a head shop. The can was hollowed out and unscrewed from the bottom. My plan was to buy the heroin from the hill tribes in Chiang Mai, and then smuggle it out of Thailand in the false-bottomed can.

I arrived in Bangkok and caught a taxi directly to Pattaya Beach. Time was the essence; I had five days left before my commitment without bail hearing. I needed an interpreter—one that I could trust. The bikini-clad babes swinging around the gold colored poles always knew where to score ganja. I just had to hope they could be trusted about heroin. For fifty bucks, I scored a bag of ganja and an escort for the week. She spoke perfect broken English. Without haste we caught the midnight bus to Chiang Mai. I revealed my plan to her on the way.

"No need go Karen tribe," she said. "I have friend Chiang Mai, he take care for you, *mai me pen ha* (no problem)."

Her friend was a taxi driver. She assured me that he could be trusted. When we got to Chiang Mai we met him in our hotel room. "Now plice velly high," he said.

"How much?" I asked, expecting to get gouged.

"One ounce, maybe five hundred dolla," he said with a grimace. I was ecstatic. I knew that it was worth up to $20,000 per ounce after cut, but had to contain my excitement.

"Ohhh," I moaned, as if it was a rip-off. "O.K., I'll take six ounces."

In a few hours, I received six ounces of CW heroin. I divided it into two socks, and stuffed them into the false-bottomed can. Everybody was happy, including my escort—after I gave her a few hundred bucks for her assistance. I left her in Chiang Mai and caught a domestic flight to Bangkok. From there, I boarded a flight to San Francisco via Honolulu with the can in my carry-on bag.

My plan was to hide each sock in separate restrooms on the airplane so I could clear Customs in Honolulu empty-handed. Hawaii, being the initial point of entry into the United States, would be the only checkpoint required. Once I was cleared, I could retrieve the stash when I re-boarded my flight to San Francisco, and walk off the plane when I got there.

Upon entering U.S. Customs in Honolulu, I was flagged and taken to secondary. I came up clean, but wasn't cleared. In a serious discussion, an older agent huddled with another agent. By his gestures, I sensed that he was ordering them to re-check the plane. Shortly afterwards, I was cleared. When I re-checked in at the gate, I was told that the flight was delayed an hour. Customs hadn't cleared it.

They found it, my gut instincts told me. I played a mental chess game as I drank a Jack Daniels on the rocks in the airport lounge. I had to figure out their strategy, if or when they found the dope. I knew that they wouldn't bust me without the dope in my possession. They would wait for me to retrieve it, so they could catch me red-handed. My new plan was to get on the plane, grab the dope, get off the plane, and hide it in the airport. Then get back on the plane, fly to San Francisco, get off empty-handed, and retrieve it later.

I had to comb the airport for a hiding place. By sheer luck, I found a hole in the cement wall of a toilet stall in the restroom. The wall appeared to be under minor renovation, and the hole opened up into a larger cavern. It was a perfect spot, and nobody would see me when I hid the stash there.

I boarded the plane an hour later. As an alibi to get on and off of the plane, I left my carry-on bag in the lounge. I immediately headed to the rear of the plane. My heart beat anxiously as I entered the first lavatory. The sock was still there. I put it into my coat pocket and hurried over to the other lavatory. It was locked with the occupied sign on. *Who could be in there already?* I wondered, as I stood outside of the stall with my hand in my pocket, holding on to the heroin filled sock.

Seemingly out of nowhere, a short mahu (gay) with a crew cut, earring and a lisp appeared. "I thee they really harrathed you in Cuthtoms," he said, trying to engage me in a conversation.

An alarmed sensation struck me. The feeling jumped in my heart. *This mahu's a Federal agent*, I thought. It was a great cover if he was. I also knew that new boarders weren't allowed on domestically connecting international flights, so I found it suspicious that I hadn't seen him during the fourteen-hour flight. It was too peculiar. I gave him the brush with a simple answer, and slipped into the crowded aisle of boarding passengers when he turned his head.

I told the stewardess that I forgot my bag in the lounge, and got off of the plane. I hid the sock in the wall of the restroom, and returned to retrieve the other sock. I told the stewardess that my friend must've taken my bag onboard, and re-boarded the plane. Halfway down the aisle, I spotted the mahu Fed through the crowd. Standing in front of his seat, directly to the right of my assigned seat, he was frantically looking around. The rest of the passengers were busy putting their bags in the overhead compartments and getting settled. This confirmed my suspicions. Cutting my losses, I left the other sock behind, and got off of the plane. I had another Jack Daniels in the lounge and watched my flight leave. Once the plane took off, I retrieved the stash from the hole-in-the-wall.

I sold most of the stash to Gordon, a local gangster who had a network of gambling and drug connections. This gave me enough money to pay my attorney fees and other debts. Two days later, I appeared in Circuit Court for my no-bail hearing. Prosecutor Carlisle got his way, and I was committed without bail for the two thefts.

[The following year, lawmakers passed a commitment without bail law for serious violent felonies. The Hawaii Supreme Court ruled it to be unconstitutional.]

A few years had lapsed since my first visit to Halawa jail. The old jail had been renovated, and the twelve-man holding tanks had been replaced with two modules, A and B. It had electronically controlled doors, three dorms within each module, and private rooms. It was luxurious compared to the old jail, yet it wasn't very comfortable for me. I didn't have a chance to smuggle in any drugs, and was forced into withdrawals. Laid up on a bunk bed, I felt like I was on my deathbed.

On the second day, an inmate who was a total stranger approached me. "Are you Andy?" he asked me.

"Yeah. Why?" I asked, disoriented and confused.

"This is for you," he said, and then passed me a note.

"If you need ANYTHING at all, let me know," it read, signed "G."

"Yeah, I need something!" I said. "Wait, who's this from?" I asked.

"Dennis told me to give it to you," he said.

"Dennis? Who's Dennis?" I asked, "And who are you? And who the f... is G," I said, thinking something funny was going on.

"Dennis is the cook. I don't know anything else," he said. "He just told me to give you this note."

It suddenly clicked. G was Gordon, the connection who I sold my stash to. He told me that he had a friend who was a civilian cook at Halawa jail. "How can I talk to Dennis?" I asked.

"I'll get you in the morning. Dennis has it all set up for you to work in the kitchen," he said simply.

While awaiting trial, I worked in the kitchen. This allowed me extra privileges, and fringe benefits. Dennis brought me Heineken, pakalolo and heroin, and I was allowed contact visits with my girlfriend. Although it was prohibited, sex in the visiting room was normal. The guards turned their heads to everything, including drugs and violence. The prisoners ran the jail. Known as the prisoner's code, the only rules were inmate rules. Violating those rules resulted in brutal punishment and protective custody (PC). Reputations are important, and drugs were a necessity. Smuggling drugs into jail boosted my reputation. I met criminals who loved drugs as much as me, and the hard-core criminals were just hard-core drug addicts. This identity bonded us. Pulling time was merely another game. The game became "us and them," addicts against the system.

The state had six months to try me on both charges; my right to a speedy trial. Two days before the trial, Prosecutor Carlisle filed a motion to continue the Kualoa set-up case. "Your honor, one of the officers was involved in a serious auto accident and his passenger died. The state would like to ask for a continuance," Carlisle asked.

"Who cares what happened to his passenger," Mirikitani argued. "There's no doctor reports saying what happened to the officer, or why he can't be here."

"Taken under advisement," Judge Hayashi decided to rule on it later. Narrowing down the fight, I knew that my speedy trial rights would assure a dismissal. The only case left hinged on the tourist from Japan. I expected another victory. Tourist weren't returned from anywhere for a $298 theft, especially from Japan.

Two days later, I returned for the trial. To my surprise, the Japanese tourists returned in a new witness-return program. I was their first test case. Aside from the prosecutor, I was the only haole in the courtroom. I felt like I was on trial for bombing Hiroshima. The victims, the judge, my attorney and the jury were all Japanese.

The stakeout team testified that they observed me with binoculars from different angles. Under cross-examination, three cops stated that they watched me stuff items into the front area of my shirt with my back to them. None of them saw me put anything into my back pocket. The arresting officer testified that he found $198 in the top left pocket of my shirt, and a hundred-dollar bill in the rear pocket of my shorts.

I didn't deny committing the theft. My defense was that I didn't take the hundred-dollar bill. To be convicted of a felony, the state had to prove that I stole over $200, whereas the $198 found in my shirt would be a misdemeanor.

"Do these look like the shorts that Andy was wearing that day?" Mirikitani asked the arresting officer, and held up the Hang Ten shorts with the front facing the officer.

"Yes," the officer affirmed.

"Which side did you recover the hundred-dollar bill from?" Mirikitani asked.

The officer searched his memory for a second. "The left side," he guessed.

Mirikitani turned the shorts around. "There's only one pocket on these shorts, and it's on the right side," he said, as he showed the jury and the officer the rear of the shorts. Carlisle cringed. We had a solid loophole to drop the case from a felony to a misdemeanor.

"If you convict him for a misdemeanor, he's going to walk out of this courtroom smiling," Carlisle said vigorously during his closing arguments. "If there were eighteen gold bars in that trunk, do you think that he'd take just one? NO! He'd take everything he could get his hands on, just like all thieves."

Deliberations lasted ten minutes. The jury convicted me for stealing $298, a felony. It became a misdemeanor when the penal code was revised a few years later. Carlisle then offered a plea deal on the remaining felony that was taken under advisement.

"The prosecutor said he'll drop the other case to a misdemeanor if you plead guilty," Mirikitani said thrilled, as if it was a fabulous deal.

I was infuriated. Held without bail was illegal, and my speedy trial rights were violated. It would be a free conviction for the prosecutor, and he'd use it against me later. "Tell him to go f... himself," I said.

"Oh, uh, okay," Mirikitani said. As I expected, the other case never came up again.

I had served eight months by the time that I was sentenced, which should've been sufficient. For the sentencing phase, the probation officer wrote several unfounded allegations in my pre-sentence report, presumably encouraged by the prosecutor, revealing the villain that I was. Jackie, my mom, appeared in court. She tried to downplay the situation. Judge Hayashi didn't buy it.

"Do you know that this is a very dangerous man here?" he scowled. "And do you think you can come in here and con the jury, Mr. Botts?" he then asked me.

Jackie doesn't take crap from anyone, and always gets the last word. "You can't send my son to prison," she retorted. "Do you know that this is E.J. Botts's grandson? And did you know...?" she rattled on.

Judge Hayashi stopped her mid-sentence with his hands up. "Hold it! I heard enough already," he said. "I was going to give him one year, but he's been in eight months already. Six months, time served," he said, and slammed his gavel before she could say more.

Carlisle was stunned. I was stoked. Thrown off by the sudden change of events, he sought a revocation for the first probation that I was put on three years earlier. He knew that Jackie was a threat, and overheard her say that she was going back to Kauai for two weeks. Carlisle rescheduled my revocation hearing a week early. I didn't find out until the day of the hearing. Jackie didn't know at all. I shouldn't have gotten any extra time for the violation, but I had a bad feeling. I wanted to continue the hearing, but Mirikitani wanted to get it over with. Against my instincts, I let him persuade me to go on with the show.

Judge Sodetani heard the revocation hearing. Tailored to his advantage, Carlisle ranted and raved over my atrocious pre-sentence report. It was his turn to win. The equivalent of being sent to San Quentin for jaywalking, I was sentenced to five years in Oahu Prison (OP) for the probation violation.

Reserved for rapists, robbers and murderers, three hundred cream-of-the-crop offenders were housed in the "Backyard" of OP. Inmate murders and escapes were common, and shakedowns always produced an abundance of drugs, guns and shanks (homemade knives). In 1972, the State Legislature approved a Correctional Master Plan and invested sixteen million dollars towards construction of Oahu Community Correctional Center (OCCC). The Master Plan was the brainchild of the University of Illinois staff members, who envisioned a unique rehabilitation community correctional center. Designed with an elaborate security process, with emphasis on "non-prison" programs, OCCC was to be the first of its kind in the nation. "The object would be to provide corrections officers with a greater variety of programs according to the individual needs of each prisoner," according to the *Honolulu Advertiser* in a December 1971 article. "A humane prison" according to this Master Plan, OCCC had thirteen red-tile roofed modules on the grounds of OP. Eight years and millions of dollars later, a transition from Oahu Prison to OCCC was underway, right when I was sentenced.

My first sixty days were spent in Module thirteen, the only module open, where I underwent a process called diagnostics. Diagnostics was a post-trial investigation to determine where I'd serve my sentence, provide recommendations on programs within the prison, and recommend possible alternatives to incarceration: probation, half-way houses, residential drug facilities, work release programs, etc. Diagnostics included a meeting with the Conditional Release Center (CRC), a prison counselor, doctor and psychiatrist.

CRC rejected me for being a drug addict. The counselor was a fat Filipino who hated criminals and haoles. The doctor was an alcoholic whose breath reeked of whiskey at 9:00 a.m., and the psychiatrist was a flaming mahu.

My orientation included a ten-minute "pep talk" with the mahu shrink. "My job is to fill out the paperwork," he informed me with a lisp. "I don't care what you tell me. If you crack your head open and you want to say 'Fell in the shower,' then I'll write, 'Fell in the shower'," he explained casually as if it was all so simple and routine. "I had one guy come in here with seven stab wounds, and he said that he fell in the shower. So I wrote 'fell in the shower.' The backyard's full of cowboys," he continued, "One day I looked out my window, and they were shooting at each other from dorm five to dorm six," he said, as he pointed towards the two-story X-shaped cellblock facing us. "I've been here fifteen years and have seen it all. Again, my job is to fill out the paperwork."

Although it was interesting to know these little facts, I didn't expect to end up in the backyard of OP. Confident that I'd be released back on probation, I continued to use drugs, and played poker throughout my diagnostic. Other inmates grabbed Bibles. Whenever volunteers were called, they were first in line; Church services, Bible studies, they were the regulars.

Brown-nosing wimps and hypocrites, I scoffed under my breath. *Rape, rob and pillage, but when you get caught you run to God.* I found it ironic how they had suddenly became holy in prison. I assumed that they weren't serious. I hadn't opened a Bible in my life, and didn't intend to then.

My prison diagnostic report was worse than my pre-sentence report. "Botts is a con-artist, professional thief and unrehabilatatable. His only placement should be in the backyard of Oahu Prison, no programs recommended." Short and sweet, this summarized their elaborate diagnostic evaluation. I was transferred to the backyard of OP.

Like being white in Harlem on a Saturday night, the backyard had less than five haoles. In Hawaii, hate crimes target haoles. It's an attitude spurred by the overthrow of the Hawaiian Monarchy by the American government. The last day of school was kill-a-haole day, so I knew what it was like to be a minority. I just didn't know what to expect in OP.

Two days earlier, inmate Francis Key was shot in the head while asleep. Francis was highly revered in the backyard. Described by the media as an underworld figure, Francis brought peace and unity between two powerful factions, the Hawaiians and the Samoans. Milton Nihipali and three other inmates shared Key's cubicle. They were arrested for suspicion of murder, and being held at the Honolulu Police Station pending an investigation.

Nihipali was feared by most, and criminally insane. He had a black patch over his right eye, and you didn't want to make eye contact with his left. Crazed with an obsession for power, with Francis dead he could run the prison. Within hours of my transfer into the backyard, Nihipali was released from the police station without charges, along with his accomplices, and returned to the backyard.

Feeling out of place, I tensely sat on a picnic table talking to a few acquaintances from the street. Nihipali came bopping out of the cellblock to use the telephone, which happened to be directly behind me. From the corner of my eye, twenty-feet away to my left, a group of muscle-bound Samoans sat on a picnic table. Dressed in jungle fatigues and combat boots, with dark glasses over their tattooed faces, they were staring directly at me. There wasn't a smile amongst them. I assumed they were staring at me because I was a haole. I refrained from making eye contact. The vibes were extremely intense. I could literally feel the hate. If there was ever a time in my life that I felt threatened, it was then. Unknown to me, it was Nihipali they were staring at, who casually talked on the phone behind me.

The backyard gradually cleared out and I found myself sitting alone. The vibes were still intense. I got up and headed back to my dorm just as Nihipali hung up the phone. As I stood at the gate waiting for the Makai'i (guard) to open it, the mob of Samoans hastily approached Nihipali. Nihipali and Clarence Freitas, another alleged accomplice in the Key murder, were immediately surrounded by the mob. I heard shouts and a few thuds. Pipes crashed down on their heads. Nihipali's throat was punctured and sliced in the method of slaughtering a pig for a luau. Blood poured onto the cement slabs of the backyard. Two Makai'is watched and waited in suspense. Within minutes it was over. The mob disbursed, and the Makai'is dragged the bodies away.

Nihipali's head hung full-tilt unto his back while they carted his body by the arms and legs to the infirmary. The medics refused to accept his butchered body. He was a goner. Nihipali's body was then taken outside to the prison parking lot. Freitas miraculously survived, but he's permanently cockeyed. One eye looks to the right, the other looks straight ahead.

The Makai'is dropped their keys and ran out the gate. A riot broke out. Every neon light was smashed, and anything not nailed down was trashed. Nobody knew that a secret meeting among the dorm leaders had been held. Nihipali was given the thumbs down, and the Samoans volunteered to do the job. To keep the secret from reaching Nihipali, nobody was told beforehand. Thought to be a factional uprising, the Samoan population was immediately segregated into the old maximum-security unit. A few weeks later, after things were sorted out, the Samoans returned to the backyard.

The inmates, known as Paahaos, sorted out problems amongst themselves. If you had a problem, you went to your dorm leader, never to the administration. Respect was mandatory among inmates. New inmates had to be sponsored into the backyard. Friends vouched for the prisoner being accepted into their dorm. They were screened by the dorm reps and had to be approved by the inmates. Problems from the street had to be quashed. Child molesters and rats went straight to PC. My reputation was considered "solid." I wasn't a rat and was well-known in the drug community. Most of all, they thought I was Portuguese. That outweighed being a haole.

The inmates ran the backyard. Heroin, cocaine, pakalolo and pills were always available, and consumed openly. Makai'is were threatened, intimidated and harassed all day long. New Makai'is rarely lasted two weeks. Women guards were no exception. I thought another riot had broken out when a female recruit was escorted through the backyard. Catcalls, whistles and every gross word imaginable erupted simultaneously from over a hundred of the sickest criminals in the islands. Most didn't make it through orientation.

A rookie Makai'i smelled the sweet scent of Hawaiian pakalolo as we blatantly passed joints around a picnic table. He couldn't believe his eyes. A handful of rolled joints sat in the middle of the table waiting to be burned. "What the f... you looking at prick?" barked Maldonado. "Turn your f...en head," he said, his way of teaching the rookie the rules.

Drugs flew over the walls in footballs when the sun went down. A twelve-foot high wall separated the backyard from Puuhale road. The weight yard, called the hobo-yard, was next to the wall. The Makai'is with rank tried to intercept the stash. Rookie

Makaiʻis didn't entertain the thought. It became a football game. The inmate who made the pick-up did a pass off. After the catch was made, the football was shoved through the bars of a dorm— touchdown; the stash was safe once inside of a dorm.

In the meantime, my family pulled strings for my release. Six months later, I returned to court on a reconsideration of sentence. As expected, Prosecutor Carlisle ranted and raved over my pre-sentence and diagnostic reports.

"Do you have anything to say, Mr. Botts?" Judge Sodetani asked me.

"Yes, your honor. This was my first time in jail and I've learned my lesson," I said humbly, knowing that the fix was in.

"You sound sincere, probation granted," he said, and thumped his gavel. Carlisle shook his head. He knew it was fixed. Unleashed to an unsuspecting public, I vowed to never return.

CHAPTER FOUR

BORN AGAIN

"Botts, grab your bags and baggage," the Makai'i called out. My baggage was a trash bag. I was injecting a shot of heroin. Mom waited at the gates. In my haze, she took me straight to the airport. We boarded a small Cessna and flew to Hanalei, Kauai, where she built an elaborate house on the golf course in Princeville.

I instantly slipped into a deep nod upon take-off, a characteristic effect of heroin intoxication. I came out of my opiate sleep as our plane approached Hanalei. Long white sandy beaches bordered the deep blue ocean. Huge surf pounded the shores. Waterfalls cascaded down the lush green mountains that disappeared into the clouds. The last thing that I remembered was the old, haunting, gray and white cement slabs of OP. It seemed as if I woke into a dream.

I fell in love with Kauai when I was sixteen years old and ran away from home. Known as the Garden Island, Kauai was very laid back and undeveloped in 1973. Traffic jams were nonexistent, and the only stoplight was in the middle of a sugarcane field. To preserve its beauty, building heights were restricted to the height of the tallest coconut tree, and still are. The local community was very friendly, close knit and trusting. So trusting that I lied about my age when I got my driver's license, and took the test without an ID. Local boy cop, local boy surfer, everybody was related. If my auntie's boyfriend's brother's wife knew your sister's boyfriend's father, we were "ohana" (family).

Hanalei is on the north shore of Kauai. *"God created the world in six days, and on the seventh he created Hanalei,"* is the saying. The hippy generation of the early seventies found Kauai's north shore. It was their Garden of Eden. Nudist colonies flourished along the north shore and into the Kalalau Valley. The Kalalau Valley's twelve-mile trail is too treacherous for the main road to encircle the island, and is accessible only by foot or boat. Unique in the Hawaiian Islands, it was a perfect location for this back-to-nature culture. Unlike the scraggly types, a lot of the hippies were attractive, clean, well proportioned young woman from mainland families. Hot chicks bathed nude in streams, walked along beaches naked, and even rode the surf butt-naked on rubber mattresses.

Times had changed by 1980. The hippies were gone and Princeville developed into a luxury community. This time I really planned to go straight. I was hired as a busboy at the Hanalei Bay Resort, overlooking Hanalei Bay. Once hired, I heard that they needed a bartender. The bar manager gave me a chance to prove myself. I trained on my own time. Within two weeks I was bartending full-time.

God fulfilled my ultimate dream in life. I lived in a luxurious house in Hanalei, surfed the best waves in the world, and bartended at night. Hard drugs didn't belong in the Garden of

Eden, but Pakalolo was still cool. Heroin was no longer a craving, until a jailhouse acquaintance wrote from Bangkok. We had exchanged addresses while I was in Halawa jail. He returned to Thailand and sent several letters filled with China White.

I seriously debated the costs of agony versus financial gain. It was the gateway to misery, but I couldn't flush it down the toilet. It was worth over $10,000. I tried to beat the odds. It was easy money at first, until my drug crave became insatiable and my connection fizzled. Out of desperation, I banged cars again.

I got busted on Kauai and bailed out. I knew that I was going back to prison, so I continued my spree. I went on to Oahu and got busted again. I couldn't believe my luck. I was on a major losing streak. I bailed out again and went on to Maui, hoping to amass enough loot to leave the state. On Maui, I scored a stack of credit cards, traveler's checks and cash, and then headed to Kahului airport. A block away from the airport, a cop waited at a sugarcane field crossroads. When he turned on his headlights and followed, I knew that he was looking for me.

I quickly shoved the stolen goods into a heater vent behind the dashboard of my rental car. The cop's blue lights started flashing. I was pulled over. I allowed him to search my car. It was my only hope of getting out of there. As expected, he didn't find the goods. A squad of cops then arrived at the scene. They assured me that I wasn't under arrest, but wanted to take me in for questioning. If I refused to go I'd be arrested. Catch-22, I followed the squad to the Wailuku Police Station.

"You could write a book on this," the Sergeant said, as he unraveled the printout of my six-foot long rap sheet like a scroll.

Just another chapter, I thought to myself.

My car was re-searched thoroughly. Twenty minutes later they found the goods. "Put him in the dungeon!" the Sergeant ordered.

The dungeon was a urine stench drunk-tank in the basement of the Wailuku police station. It had no toilets. To use the restroom, I had to knock on the roof of the cell. The knocks went unanswered. As seemed to be the norm, I urinated in the corner. Huddled under an army blanket that reeked of puke, I endured another harsh jones. The following day was my twenty-fifth birthday. I expected to be retired by then. It was my standard line. Instead, I was stuck in a dungeon. Determined to spend my birthday anywhere else, I had to figure a way out of there.

Two Maui cops escorted me to the Detective's division the following morning. It was a relief to see the sky and breathe fresh air. I could taste freedom. My mind was in escape mode as they led me to the opposite side of the police station. Near the entrance of the Detective's division, we passed a restroom with glass-louvered windows. It was my best if not only chance.

They led me into a partitioned cubicle to be questioned by a detective. On his desk was an evidence envelope with the confiscated goods. The detective fed me hot coffee and doughnuts. The old good cop routine, he expected a confession. I played along with his game. When he turned his back, I stole $100 from the evidence envelope.

"Can I use the bathroom?" I asked, ready for my break. He took me to a windowless restroom instead of the glass-louvered one. I was discouraged, but had to keep trying. Whenever the detective left his cubicle, a different cop watched me. I continued trying, but they kept taking me to the windowless restroom. On my fifth try, the windowless restroom was finally occupied.

"Can you wait?" the cop asked me, as we stood outside of the restroom.

"No man, I gotta shit real bad!" I said with a serious look, holding my okole desperately with both hands. After thinking about it for a second, he took me to the restroom with glass louvers. Not wanting to smell the aroma, he waited outside of the door. I locked the door between us.

Within seconds, the louvers were out and I was gone. I frantically ran down the street panic-stricken. I didn't know what to do. My mind had been in escape mode, but I didn't have a plan after that. A taxi would be my quickest exit. I knocked on the door of the first house in sight. An old Japanese lady answered the door. The desperation in my demeanor was obvious. She was uneasy, but allowed me to use her phone to call a cab.

My heart beat rapidly as I hid in a mango tree and waited for the taxi. The cab arrived and took me to Kaanapali Beach, on the opposite side of the island. Half-way there, my escape was broadcast over the car's radio, "Tall, slim, 135 pounds, wearing blue jeans and a bamboo print shirt." The cabbie eyed me in his rear view mirror. I fit the description. I thought he'd turn me in. Instead, he took me to the Royal Lahaina Hotel. Sparingly, I gave him $5.00, and promised to be back with the rest of the $50.00 fare in a minute. I entered the hotel, dashed through the lobby, and then sprinted down the beach to the Sheraton Maui.

To change my appearance, I bought a pair of swim shorts and an Aloha shirt from the Sheraton hotel's gift shop. To wash off the stench of the dungeon, I dove into the hotel's swimming pool. After a quick birdbath, I forged the guest list for a beach towel. Lounging poolside with a cold Heineken, I contemplated my next move. I assumed that the cabbie would call the cops, especially after getting stiffed. It wouldn't be long before the posse would show up.

My sister Sybil lived on Molokai, the island closest to Maui. I called her and asked to borrow money. I told her that I lost my wallet and was stuck on Maui. Instead of sending money, she offered to fly down with her husband in his Cessna airplane. Unfortunately, they could only land at Kahului Airport, on the side of the island where I had escaped. *A crook always returns to the scene of the crime*, I thought to myself, concerned that a manhunt would be on at Kahului airport.

My only option, I hailed another cab. I looked like a tourist with my new clothes and shopping bag. I had my dirty clothes in the shopping bag. Imitating a southern accent, I told the cabby that I needed to pick-up a friend at the airport, and that it would be a round-trip. The cabbie didn't have a clue. He'd make his day on my fare. In route to the airport, a squad of cops blazed past us. I started to feel at ease. The manhunt was heading in the opposite direction.

When we pulled into the airport, I spotted my sister's red and white Cessna coming in for a landing. To avoid suspicion, I left the shopping bag of dirty clothes in the taxi and promised to be right back. Aboard their plane before the propellers had a chance to stop, we flew off into the sunset.

It was dark by the time that we reached Molokai. The phone rang as we entered their house. I knew that it was my mother calling. By the sound of the conversation, I could sense that she already knew about my latest stunt. We sat down for dinner and her children said grace. They were Christians. Something touched me emotionally. I felt a spiritual goodness within their household and was suddenly flooded with tears.

My sister and brother-in-law confronted me after dinner and confirmed that Mom had called. Their advice was to turn myself in. It was an absurd idea. I'd definitely go back to prison for a long time. My only foreseeable hope was to stay on the run for five years, until the statute of limitations ran out.

I called my mother in the morning and wished her a happy birthday. She returned the same. Her birthday is November 18, mine is November 19. "Well it's my twenty-fifth birthday, I guess this means I'm retired," I said. "Sybil wants me to turn myself in. What do you think?" I asked her.

"No way, don't be a damned fool," she said, which is what I wanted to hear. "Just relax and take it easy awhile. They'll never find you on Molokai."

It seemed like a good idea, until the cops showed up at my brother-in-law's job site later that day. I couldn't jeopardize them for harboring a fugitive, so I turned myself in. I was arrested at his job site and flown back to Maui. Charged with escape and numerous thefts, I was detained at the Maui Jail.

Prior to being placed into the main population, I was kept in solitary confinement pending a physical. I reflected on my life and the numerous coincidences that I had experienced. My life was so abnormal that I could've died and it wouldn't have mattered to me. I wished I could start it over again, like a child. *If this is life God, then you can have it. I want no part of it. Either take this life or give me a new one*, I prayed. I didn't know that such a prayer was possible. It was how I felt in my heart.

The following day I moved into the main population and attended a Christian fellowship, another first for me. It was then that I dedicated my life to Jesus Christ. Amid a flood of tears, I immediately felt the Holy Spirit fill the void of life that was missing. A harmonious purr enveloped me. My fears were replaced with peace, contentment and joy. "I was blind, but now I see," suddenly made sense.

I started to read the Bible. It gave me a deeper understanding of life, but I was unsure of the supernatural stories. The prediction of Christ's birth being foreseen by three astronomers from the East (the three wise men) was debatable. Dreams, visions and miraculous powers were even harder to swallow. I assumed that the stories were exaggerated, until I experienced them myself.

I had an unusual dream that was as vivid as a movie. The dream was vague at first. The cops were chasing me. It seemed as though I was getting arrested. I could feel the sensation of being arrested as if it was an actual experience. *How could I be getting arrested, I asked myself. It's impossible; I'm already in jail.*

In the next moment, I was standing in the Police Station. A document that looked like a police report faced away from me on the desk. The clarity was concise. I was looking down at the document and could clearly see five charges typed on it. Suddenly,

I was shaking hands with a cop. *This is totally crazy. I would never shake hands with a cop,* I thought to myself, and then woke-up.

I couldn't get it out of my mind when I woke up. It was too bizarre to be true, yet it seemed so real, so I told my cellmates about it. Within minutes of relating my dream to them, a guard entered the dayroom. "Botts, put on your shirt, you're going for a re-booking," he said.

"Re-booking? What's a re-booking?" I asked.

"You've been indicted," he explained, "Everyone gets re-booked after they're indicted on Maui."

I knew the system well, but this was something new to me. In Honolulu you get booked and then go to jail, end of story. I was handcuffed by a Maui cop and taken to the Wailuku police station. As I stood in the booking area, I looked down at what appeared to be the indictment lying on the Sergeant's desk. Facing in the opposite direction, I saw five charges typed in bold letters, exactly as I had dreamt. It was uncanny, but I've seen my share of coincidences, so I wasn't sure.

The Maui cop was a super-cool Hawaiian. When he mugged and fingerprinted me, he noticed that I lived in Kailua. Coincidently, he was from Waimanalo, the town bordering Kailua, and used to bang cars also. He explained that he got married and moved to Maui to get out of the game. We also knew a lot of the same people, including his cousin Danny, who was my partner when I lived in San Francisco. We were both amazed. A friendship bonded. I couldn't make long distance calls at the Maui jail, so he let me call my family on the outer islands.

When we returned to the Maui jail, he didn't handcuff me afterwards, despite the fact that I had escaped from them. Spontaneously, I shook his hand in gratitude. When our hands clasped, I was struck with a distinct déjà vu feeling. *WOW*, I thought as I flashed back to my dream, *I'm actually shaking a cop's hand.*

Additionally, the prison doors have opened for me in peculiar ways. Within a month, I was transferred to Oahu prison for an outstanding misdemeanor charge. Bail was set at $30,000 on Maui, while bail on the misdemeanor was $50.00.

"What Botts, you no more the $50.00 for bail?" the housing officer asked me when I got there. He didn't see the $30,000 bail hold posted on the back of the misdemeanor bail order. I immediately realized his error, but didn't have any cash on me. I tried to call my father, but couldn't get an outside line because of the over-used phone lines in OCCC. I was frustrated. I could've been released for a measly fifty bucks. However, knowing that everything happens for a reason, I realized that I would've been released if it were meant to be. God had other plans for me.

A year later, Oahu Prison became OCCC. The inmates in the backyard of OP were disbursed amongst the thirteen modules. I was in Module thirteen, a unit designed for work furloughs— a program that never got implemented. A computer in the main control booth, including a back door that led directly to the main street, controlled all doors. I just happened to be standing by this back door when Hurricane Iwa hit Hawaii in 1982. A bolt of lightning flashed and thunder vibrated the module. In an unprecedented power shortage, the lights went out for ten seconds. The cell doors, including this back door, all clicked open simultaneously. On impulse I turned to push open the door. A conviction of doubt suddenly enveloped me. *Is it meant to be?* I asked myself. This time I resisted the urge.

I was sentenced to ten years for possession of two credit cards, double the max as a repeat offender. The parole board set a minimum term of six years before parole. On the remaining charges, including the escape, I was sentenced to five years on each. The sentences were consolidated and ran concurrently.

The only programs available were the ones that I created. I read the Bible, took courses in accounting, and created an exercise routine. The Holy Spirit instilled an ambitious desire to change my life, and a desire to help others. I became an English tutor and taught other inmates. Yet, I didn't know what a verb was until then. By teaching I learned. I also had access to a typewriter and learned how to type.

The illiteracy level among young adults was sad. Many were Hawaiians handicapped in skills and opportunities. Like me, they were stuck in the cycle of drug and alcohol addiction. It's what they learned. Unless they learned a new program, they ended up back in the system or homeless. The authorities didn't seem to care if they were released without a job, house, money or support. Yet, when they failed and returned to prison it was their fault. It was an injustice that burned me up.

A friend turned me on to a creative idea as I watched him type business letters. "What are you doing?" I asked curiously.

"I'm writing my way out of prison," he said simply.

"Writing your way out?" I chuckled, "What do you mean?"

"Just what I said," he replied. "I'm not going to sit around for the next ten years just because they told me so. I'm writing to various companies, the parole board, and even the governor if I have to. I've got positive ideas that'll help the community and a parole plan when they release me," he said.

It made sense, so I started to write my way out. After serving almost two years, a community service program was established by Tom Hugo, the Chairman of the Hawaii Paroling Authority. It was a three to six month program. Through this program, we could earn work furlough privileges or parole. I wrote three persuasive letters: one to Hugo, another to the administrator, and the other to Sgt. Randy Asher who oversaw the crew.

Out of over a thousand inmates, I was chosen to be one of twenty prisoners on the full-time crew. I was also the only repeat offender, which they didn't realize until later. The work was tough and I was the scrawniest guy on the chain gang. Sgt. Asher and Hugo didn't think I'd last a week. Grateful for the opportunity, I worked extra hard. For twenty-five cents an hour, we chopped trees and cleared brush between the Pali Lookout and Kailua, my hometown. It was intense training, but rewarding. Instead of sitting in a cell watching TV all day, we were outside giving back to the community. Car horns honked in support. My friends shouted, "Free Andy." As a reward, we were taken to the beach once a month. My friends were the lifeguards.

"Were you the Mayor of this town or something?" Sgt. Asher asked, after using the restroom at a gas station in Kailua. The gas station attendant was my classmate.

Everything was working out perfectly. It was during this time that I discovered another unusual phenomenon when I played backgammon with Jerry. It started out as fun, until he couldn't beat my streak. I boasted that I was the luckiest guy in the world, which was my only explanation. Jerry didn't buy it. Instead, he persuaded me into playing for a ten-cent bag of potato chips. I usually don't gamble, especially in prison, because it's a no-win situation. If I win, I lose, because I hate to take money from prisoners. If I lose, they're quick to grab my money. It's a game of greed. A ten-cent bet seemed harmless though.

The stakes went up as Jerry chased the odds to break even. It seemed like a lucky streak, but I knew better. I tried to warn him, but he wouldn't listen. It's a feeling of invincibility that coincides with my intuition. I knew what the roll would be before rolling the dice. As the dice hit the table, I called out the numbers. On command, the dice seemingly obeyed. This happened so often that it defied odds, yet Jerry continued to chase the odds. From a ten-cent bet, he lost a thousand dollars. I knew that it wasn't a fluke, because I had a similar experience prior to this.

My partner Danny, the Maui cop's cousin, was a superstitious gambler who believed that omens portended good luck streaks. After having diarrhea all night, he was overcome with this "omen." We immediately drove several hundred miles to Reno to cash in on his lucky diarrhea streak. He must've had the runs on my behalf though.

It was my first time in a casino. I had just turned twenty-one. After walking around the tables at Harrah's, I settled on a roulette table that I felt comfortable with. Whether it was the table or the mystically sexy redhead spinning the wheel I'm not sure. It was just a confident feeling that I sensed. I had a wad of hundred dollar bills in my wallet. I wasn't prepared to throw them away though. Instead, I pulled out two twenty-dollar bills. This was spare change that I expected to lose.

My mind was relaxed as I watched the wheel spin. I envisioned a serene surf spot on Kauai as I stared at the white ball circling the perimeter. In a trance-like state, consciously I was in the casino, subconsciously I wasn't. The noise in the casino disappeared, but the rattling sound of the white ball got louder. Suddenly, a specific number overshadowed the visual that I focused on. I knew that it was the winning number. I bet a stack of chips on every spot that coincided with this number. "Seventeen!" I shouted, and snapped my fingers with certainty. The white ball landed into slot number seventeen.

Pretty lucky, I thought, but after awhile I started to wonder. The numbers kept popping into my head. I called a dozen numbers correctly. The redhead spinning the wheel was amazed. She blinked her eyes. When it was an odd number, I bet everything. When I saw an even number, I wouldn't bet at all. It's something about odd numbers or odd things that intrigue me, and this was one of those odd things. Within half an hour, I was up over $1000, after tipping the redhead several hundred dollars. Occasionally I guessed wrong, and quit when I lost twice in a row. I took it as a sign and walked away from the table.

From a logical perspective, I believe that my mind calculated the speed of the wheel and ball like a computer. In fact, if the mind created computers, then it's greater than a computer. When

I eliminated the physical distractions from my consciousness, the combination of intuition and subconscious calculation flowed. I believe that greed disrupts this capability though, which is why gamblers lose when they chase the odds.

I returned to Harrah's six months later, and the redhead was working again. "Hey, you're the guy who was here before!" she exclaimed when she recognized me. I just smiled and tried my luck again. It felt different this time. I wasn't on, so I walked away from the table.

After six months on the chain gang, I paid my dues according to what had been promised. I could taste freedom. However, the counselors turned down my requests for furlough or early parole. I was their hardest worker, yet I was the only one left from the original crew. I didn't see it as God's plan. We had a deal and they reneged. I became discouraged.

A friend passed by in his car and threw me a joint while we were working. It was a perfect time to give in. *Just one time won't hurt*, I rationalized. A drug test was ordered that afternoon and I was sent back to prison. They gave me thirty days in the hole and raised my security level. I was devastated. It was my only chance for an early release.

The hole consisted of twelve, six by ten dark green cells, lined side by side. The doors were iron-barred electric gates. A stainless steel toilet-sink bolted to the rear of the cell. A three by five metal cot protruded from the wall. Cold and barren, nothing was allowed in the cell other than a mattress, blanket, towel and Bible.

Times had changed. OCCC was triple capacity, and the prisoners no longer controlled the prison. The Attorney General ordered a major shakedown in December of 1981. In a show of power, the police force, National Guard, and every prison guard participated in a five-day shakedown and shake-up. Every prisoner was beaten mercilessly, five at a time. Investigations dragged on for years. Prisoners, supported by the American Civil Liberties Union (ACLU) and the U.S. Justice Department, filed a class-action lawsuit. The ACLU cited OCCC as the worst prison in the United States. The allegations didn't faze the staff. Instead, they continued to rob the facility blind, assault prisoners, and rape the female inmates. The hole was a prime example of their attitude.

Joey was housed in cell one. He was segregated from the population for his protection (PC). Joey was let out of his cell to shower for fifteen minutes every morning. Left unsupervised, Joey took the comic section from the newspaper that the Makaiʻi left between the bars. When the Makaiʻi returned, Joey tossed the comics to Randy in cell five. Of all places to land, they fell short and landed in front of my cell.

After Joey was re-locked in, I grabbed the comics and tried to pass them to Randy. My electric gate immediately slid open. "Where's the paper Botts?" the Makaiʻi asked, after he walked over to my cell.

"Oh this," I said, smiling, hoping he wouldn't make a big deal of it.

After finishing my thirty days in the hole, I was held pending an investigation for the comics. Five days later, I was charged with five ludicrous violations, ranging from unauthorized property to possession of an officer's clothing or equipment. It was as if I had stolen a guard's gun and made a break for it. Joey was charged with theft. Randy was charged with blackmail and extortion, all from the same comics. The disciplinary hearings, known as the kangaroo courts, were held within view of our cells, to the left of cell one. The counselor and two large goons made up the court.

Joey was called out first. He was to testify against us. "No way! I can't do that," Joey protested.

The counselor slapped him, and the goons pounced on him. His head was slammed into the bars. Joey dropped and flopped on the ground in convulsions. The prison paramedic was called in and tried to revive him. After twenty minutes of flopping, Joey was taken out on a stretcher.

"Next hearing, Botts," the goons called out. My cell door cranked open. Fearing the worst, I came out of my cell apprehensively and approached the kangaroo court. One goon stood to my left, the other to my right. I could smell the garlic as they breathed down my neck. The counselor read out the charges.

"How do you plead?" snarled the goons. I couldn't think, nor could I plead guilty. I'd get more time in the hole and it'd affect my security. I could never work my way out again. I tried to explain the circumstances. "How do you plead?" they said impatiently, louder this time.

"I don't know," I said nervously, "Not guilty I guess."

I was found guilty on all charges. Due to my "refusal to confess and plead guilty," they sentenced me to thirty more days in the hole, no credit for the five days spent during the investigation. I spent a total of sixty-five days in the hole. It never seemed to end. The hole was my monastery. I read the Bible and meditated in prayer for hours on end. Prior to this, I had drifted away from that routine. It was easy to go astray, even in prison. It became a practice that I found valuable for spiritual intensification. I felt in tune spiritually and had another lucid dream—a vivid nightmare.

From a quarter of a mile away, an old black locomotive slowly chugged along under the cover of night. An intense feeling of fear enveloped me. It traveled from my left towards my right, and then turned towards me. My heart beat hard and fast. *Why is this train so scary?* I self-talked to myself. *We don't have trains in Hawaii. So what's with the train? Does it signify something?* It slowly chugged closer. My heart beat harder. I sensed that I'd be in prison for a long time—about ten years. My heart sank. I felt doomed. I thought that I'd serve my entire ten-year sentence. Suddenly, my younger sister Claudia's face appeared for a few seconds. "Don't worry, everything's going to be O.K.," she said, with a smile of optimism.

No way, it's not O.K, something is seriously wrong! I thought, as the train continued getting closer. It finally reached me. It was right up to my face. The shrill of the train's whistle blasted me out of my nightmare. I bolted upright out of my sleep. My shirt was completely soaked in sweat. My heart continued to beat wildly. It freaked me out. I didn't know what to make of it. It seemed so real that I still remember it clearly to this day.

I became concerned about my future. I met a lot of prisoners who were devout Christians in prison, but backslid and fell into the old cycle when released. I couldn't understand it. Chaplain Rick seemed to have the answers.

"Hey Chaplain, what's the deal with John?" I called out to him as he made his daily rounds. John was one of the Chaplain's assistants. He faithfully followed the Lord for ten years, and then went out and pulled an armed robbery within a few months.

"Read Philippians 1:6," he replied, as if it was a common question.

"Being confident of this, that he who began a good work in you will carry it on to completion until the day of Christ Jesus," I read, memorized, and still think about.

My only hope for an early release would be through the courts. I could accept a sentence of five years for my crimes, but having a six-year minimum on a non-violent crime was ridiculous. I prayed to have the extended term on my sentence dropped, and hit the law books when I got out of the hole. I found a relief used in challenging illegal sentences, called a Rule-40 motion. It was a shot in the dark, but it was my only shot.

Within six months, a hearing was granted. My motion was based on ineffective assistance of counsel and an illegal sentence. The court appointed an attorney who was a Christian. I knew that God was in control. To confirm my testimony, he sent in an expert on conversions.

During my hearing, the prosecutor objected to the grounds raised in my motion. After reviewing the facts, Judge Marie Milks ruled in his favor and dismissed my motion. In an unexpected twist, she examined my institutional record and granted a reconsideration of sentence. Citing that I "made good on a bad situation," she dropped the extended term imposed on me as a career criminal. My sentence was reduced from ten years to five. I was discharged on my thirtieth birthday.

CHAPTER FIVE

SEX, MONEY, AND GREED

"You're Andy Botts?" she asked elatedly, which I should've taken as a sign. Nicole was a tall and gorgeous, twenty-seven year old Japanese-Caucasian mix, known as hapa-haole. I met her when I ran into an old friend. I lived on Maui, but was in Honolulu for the weekend. I had tickets to a Billy Ocean concert, so I asked her out. She accepted my invitation without hesitation. I was thrilled.

The concert was two weeks away, so I flew back to Maui. During that time, I met a pretty local Japanese girl on Maui. She was a divorcee who lived in a cozy country house on a two-acre spread. I took her out to dinner at the Hyatt Regency Maui. After dinner, we snuck into a grass shack that was roped-off with a keep-out sign posted. I thought it was a safe place to roll a joint. She thought it was the best place to give me a blowjob. After five years in prison, how could I object? Falling in lust, she was just what I wanted. We dated for the next two weeks.

I flew back to Honolulu and kept my date with Nicole. While at the Billy Ocean concert, I ran into Brent. He just happened to be in town for the week. Brent was an athletic local haole with a square jaw and short blond curly hair. We grew up together in Kailua and had our share of mischief as kids. He now lived in San Diego and was an auto wholesaler. I planned to spend Christmas with my family in San Francisco, so I promised to look him up afterwards.

After the concert, Nicole and I went out on the town. We had a fabulous evening together. She told me that she was a Christian. I was ashamed to admit that I was too. I wasn't going to church at the time, but should've been. I didn't know where to go. In prison it's easy. A church is always there. This was a new program. I knew that I needed a Christian girl to keep me on the right track though, and she was exactly what I prayed for.

Now I had to choose. It was either the hot date on Maui, or the Christian who didn't believe in sex before marriage. I struggled with the decision. The Lord put me back on my feet; I thought I could take it from there. Thirty years old, fresh out of prison, I made my choice with the wrong head. I moved in with the girl on Maui.

In the prime of my life, tan and healthy, I was now a journeyman carpenter in Hawaii's Carpenter Union. Using my carpentry skills, I built a porch and garage for her house. Every morning, we sat on the porch and drank fresh mint tea, while we watched the sunrise behind Haleakala. Living my life for the world and everything in it, I returned to surfing, and smoked killer-diller, sixty-day African hash buds that I grew in the backyard. What I considered an envious life, I couldn't complain. I can imagine Saint Lucifer snickering though. My girlfriend was turned off whenever I spoke about Christianity. "She had met too many phony Christians," as she put it, which is a common and unfortunate misconception. Christianity isn't about believing and trusting in Christians. It's believing, trusting and having faith in Jesus Christ.

I spent Christmas with my family in San Francisco. After Christmas, I visited Brent in San Diego. Brent seemed to be doing well in the auto business. He sold me a BMW and Kharman Ghia for $1000 each. I shipped them back to Honolulu, sold both immediately, and doubled my investment.

Fascinated by fast money made legally, I started to visit Brent regularly. We went to Mexico a few times, rode four-wheelers on the sand dunes, drank Margaritas in the hot sun, and enjoyed life on our terms. Things got bigger and better. Brent laid out a scheme that could net us $100,000 legally. The plan was to buy late model, low-mileage autos from the rental agencies in Hawaii. Massive fleet reductions are held every year, and thousands of cars are sold below wholesale price to dealers. Brent had a connection with one of the head honchos of the fleet sales, but had less than $20,000 to invest. Money was the only obstacle. He was told to come back when he had at least $100,000. Brent suggested we make a drug run.

I thought it over. The auto business was a lucrative trade, and the scheme was viable. If we had the capitol and invested it legally, we would be set. $100,000 wasn't worth the risk though. Brent assured me that he could double it in a snap, which he emphasized with a snap of his fingers. After serious contemplation, I considered every angle to beat the odds.

"Getting it, bringing it in, and selling it isn't the hard part. The only obstacle that we're facing is greed," I told him, "Because if you do it once, then you'll want to do it a million times. If we go, we've got to get in, make the money, and then get out." Figuring in the greed factor, I upped the ante. "Tell me how much is enough, one million, two million? Tell me now, because it's a one-time deal. One time, and one time only," I said decisively.

Brent insisted on $100,000. I knew otherwise. For argument's sake, I doubled his figure to $200,000, so he couldn't say it wasn't enough later. Agreed upon, we shook hands and the deal was sealed. I'd arrange the purchase and manage the sales. Brent would mule the stash back through San Francisco.

My girlfriend on Maui didn't object when she knew how much money would be made. With her blessings, I flew off to Bangkok. As a cover, Brent and his fiancée toured through Japan and Hong Kong on their way to Bangkok. This gave me time to purchase a pound of heroin and tour Thailand, starting from Pattaya Beach.

Pattaya had changed little over the last eight years. Michael Jackson and Madonna blared from the loudspeakers of go-go bars. Masses of European and Middle-easterners crammed the strip. Women of every size, shape, and age beckoned for me to sit with them. Amidst a crowd of lost souls hoping to fulfill their fantasies, I couldn't help wonder who the sex slave was. After hanging out for a few days, I went into the Baby a go-go club for a drink, and only a drink.

Margarita slid up to me seductively and slipped her arm over my shoulder. "Hi Daddy," she giggled, and that's all she wrote. Tall, slim and perfectly shaped, similar to a Hawaiian-Chinese mix, I bought her a Margarita, her new name, and left with the hottest chick in Thailand.

From Pattaya, we caught a taxi to Koh Samui port. A large ferryboat transported us to Koh Samui Island. Koh Samui simulated a South Pacific resort with palm thatched beach bungalows. Feeling right at home, I lounged in the shade of an open-air Polynesian-type restaurant, drank a cold Heineken and rolled a joint. Pot was legal there. I scored a bag of weed from my waiter and ate a stack of ganja-laden pancakes. On the beach, twenty feet away, Margarita sunbathed topless in her skimpy white G-string bikini bottom. Afterwards, I joined her on the beach.

An Italian dude drooled while I massaged Margarita's golden tan with coconut oil. A stunning olive skinned Italian chick lay by his side. "Did she come from Hawaii with you?" he asked, with the look of lust in his eyes.

"No, she's Thai," I said casually. "Why? Do you want to borrow her?" I asked. He grinned. The Italian chick glared.

From Koh Samui, we flew to Chiang Mai. Eight years had lapsed since my last run. I had to find a new connection. The Golden Triangle always had loads of China White. The hill tribes seemed to be the best source. Hill-treks into the opium fields became a tourist attraction. Under the guise of sightseeing, we planned a hill-trek into the mountains above Chiang Mai. With Margarita as a translator, we caught a taxi to Doi Suthep temple. Impersonating a lost tourist, I strolled around and took pictures while Margarita negotiated our expedition into the jungles.

In the back of a canvas-covered 4-wheel drive Toyota truck, we were driven to the Karen village. The dense forested route hadn't changed. An older tribesman approached us as we got out of the truck. "You want smoke opium?" he asked openly.

"Yeah, sure," I said excited, hopeful to score heroin as easily.

We followed him into a bamboo palm thatched hut. I smoked several bowls of opium while Margarita negotiated the deal with "Charlie." Charlie was a nickname adopted from American GI's during the Vietnam War. I just wondered if he knew that Charlie was also the name for the Viet Cong. Charlie needed to arrange the purchase, so we returned the following day.

I purchased a pound of nearly pure heroin when we met, and packed it into four false-bottomed toiletry cans. I had to smuggle it back to Bangkok, where I planned to meet Brent. To be safe, Margarita suggested we catch the midnight train to Bangkok. Up to then, I didn't know there was a train.

When the black locomotive pulled into the Chiang Mai station, I recognized a definite familiarity that stopped me in my tracks. I instantly flashed back to the nightmare that I had in OP. It was identical to the train in my nightmare. As if looking face to face with the devil, the train's round face above its accordion grill projected a menacing smile. An apprehensive feeling overcame me. It seemed to be a warning. Tickets in hand, it was too late to change our plans.

The midnight train to Bangkok was a seven-hour ride. In route, I thought about my previous nightmare. The similarity seemed to be so ironic. When we arrived safely the following morning, I shrugged off my inclinations as being superstitious and paranoid. Expecting Brent and his fiancée's arrival, I gave Margarita a few hundred bucks to keep her quiet, and sent her on her way.

Everything seemed to be going smoothly when I met Brent and his fiancée at the Bangkok Hilton. Concealed in separate toiletry bags, two cans each, I gave them the heroin filled cans. They returned to San Francisco the day after me and breezed through U.S. Customs. Unfortunately, my return to Honolulu wasn't as uneventful.

My last run had been in 1979, when I gave the mahu Fed the slip. While waiting for Brent, I re-acquired a heroin habit. To avoid a jones in route, I concealed a gram of heroin into the inside seam of my wallet. My wallet had never been searched in the past, and I didn't think they'd bother me after eight years. Instead of an aisle seat as I was assured, I got a window seat, and spent the entire flight stuck on the inside of a weird couple. Next to me was a Burmese lady who could've been a hand grenade juggler from the Rangoon circus. She had stubs for hands. A thumb and baby finger protruded from her right stub, and her left hand was a fingerless fist. Her haole boyfriend couldn't have been weirder. He had a gross pale face, with an ogle of perversion written on it. A match made in hell, they drank obsessively when we took off, and then slept the rest of the flight. Whenever I needed to use the restroom, I had to climb over them. To overcome the monotony of my flight, I consumed a generous amount of heroin in the restroom.

When I entered U.S. Customs in Honolulu, I was immediately taken to secondary. I was strip-searched, my wallet was checked, and everything that I purchased in Thailand was X-rayed. They didn't find the gram in my wallet. Ironically, the Customs agent that searched me was from Kailua.

"C'mon Andy," he pleaded, "I used to go to all of your parties. I know you like to make fast money. If you've got anything give it to me."

"C'mon man, I'm not that stupid," I said. "Besides that I probably make more money than you. I'm a journeyman carpenter in the Hawaii Carpenters Union."

After a thorough inspection, I expected to be cleared. The head agent then approached and asked to see my plane ticket. "Can I ask you a few questions, Mr. Botts?" he asked, after he looked at my ticket.

"Yeah sure, what do you want to know?" I said.

"Can you come with me?" he asked, just as the lady with stubs was escorted past us.

"Are they bothering you too?" she asked me. "I was already cleared and walking out the door, and they brought me back in."

I didn't answer. I was still annoyed from sitting next to her throughout the flight. Instead, I shrugged my shoulders and followed the agent to a back office behind the luggage carousel.

He brought in a local Japanese agent who was probably their top inspector. The lining of every shirt and garment was searched meticulously, and everything that I bought in Thailand was X-rayed again. I thought that they were harassing me for giving the mahu Fed the slip in 1979. After awhile, I became irritated.

"I thought you said you wanted to ask me some questions," I said to the head agent. "Go ahead, shoot." He ignored me.

I flipped open my passport and held it up to his face so he could read the inner page. "**THE SECRETARY OF STATE OF THE UNITED STATES OF AMERICA HEREBY REQUESTS ALL OF WHOM IT MAY CONCERN TO PERMIT THE CITIZEN NATIONAL OF THE UNITED STATES OF**

AMERICA MENTIONED HEREIN TO PASS WITHOUT DELAY OR HINDRANCE."

"I'm an American citizen and I know my rights. You have no right to detain me," I said. "Either charge me or release me immediately," I demanded.

"We're detaining you for conspiracy to import heroin into the United States of America," he said, with a serious look on his face.

Brent hadn't left Bangkok yet, so I took it as a bluff. "Conspiracy! Conspiracy your F...en ass," I snapped back, "It takes two or more to make a conspiracy, and I'm traveling alone. Who the F... am I supposed to be conspiring with?"

"Well, how come those people in the front are asking how much your bail is then?" he asked.

"F... you!" I said, with my middle finger projected a few inches from his face. "Nobody knows I'm in this F...en building right F...en now, except for me and F...en you," I shouted, as I pointed my index finger at him.

He was enraged, but I was right. He didn't say another word. Instead, he walked over to the Japanese inspector. "I told you to look for one thing and one thing only," he ordered. The inspector just glared back at him. Without thinking, the head agent thumbed through some clothes that were already inspected.

"I check already. You want to check huh?" the Japanese inspector said.

I chuckled while they argued with each other. To add fuel to the fire, I laid down on the carpet in the corner. "Hey can you give me a pillow?" I teased, "Just wake me up when you're done, O.K?"

"Get up, get up," the head agent ordered testily. "Where's your wallet?" he asked. I pulled out my wallet and gave it to him. He searched it, but didn't find the stash. Afterwards, he put the wallet on the counter. When he wasn't looking, I picked it up and put it back into the inside pocket of my suit.

A while later he realized that my wallet wasn't on the counter. He demanded it again. He searched it once more, but still didn't find the stash. "Leave it there and don't touch it again," he ordered, and slapped the wallet on the desk.

"Why don't you just look up my asshole so I can go home," I said, hoping he'd give up. Instead, the search went on for over two hours. The Japanese inspector was the only one left in the room by then. I started to have a bad feeling about the stash. Due to his thoroughness, I had a hunch that he would find it. I needed to get rid of it. Acting thirsty, I asked for a glass of water. I was given a Styrofoam cup of water. I nursed it while debating my options. I thought about picking up the wallet and pulling out the bindle. I wanted to dunk it in the water, but didn't want to get caught pulling it out of my wallet. Maybe he wouldn't find it, I hoped, so I decided to wait and see.

The inspector completed his search, stood up, and looked around. He spotted the wallet on the counter. Not expecting anything, he walked over and picked it up. I stood next to him with the cup of water in my hand as he looked through it. Carefully squeezing the seams, he felt the slight lump and pulled out the bindle. "What's this?" he asked, holding out the bindle of smack. He didn't know what it was. I didn't know what to do.

"I don't know," I said nonchalantly, shrugging my shoulders.

"What is it?" I asked, and feigned a curious look on my face. My heart skipped beats. I had to think fast. He slowly opened the bindle in front of my face. My heart dropped when a thick pile of white powder was exposed. I threw the water in his face, grabbed the bindle of smack, shoved it into my mouth, and ran out the door. My glands salivated from the strong sour taste of heroin as I sprinted towards the restroom. I had to flush it.

"Stop him! Stop him! I found it," the inspector shouted as he chased me. Japanese tourists standing by the luggage carousels froze. The room became silent. Time stood still. Floorwalkers appeared out of nowhere, racing towards me from all angles. I wouldn't make it to the toilet. I grabbed a plastic rubbish can on wheels, spit the dope into it, and simultaneously rolled it into the bull charging towards me. He fell over the can. Blind to the agent on my tail, a football tackle brought me down in a thud. My face was pressed into the cement. I was handcuffed behind my back and taken into another room for interrogation.

A huge poi-fed Hawaiian-Chinese gorilla entered the room. "What the F... you think you're doing punk?" he said.

"F... you, I wasn't born yesterday," I retorted, "I know when I'm being set-up," I said indignantly. Not sure what to believe, he walked out of the room confused. I never saw him again.

I was booked for heroin trafficking, and interrogated for several hours. They thought that I was connected with the strange Burmese girl. It turned out that she had fifty grams of heroin in her snatch. They promised to let me go if I told on her. They didn't believe that I didn't know her. I couldn't believe it either. I spent over six hours in Customs trying to convince them.

"Look man, I don't know what to tell you," I finally said. "I mean I've got dope, she's got dope, we're sitting next to each other, even I wouldn't believe me. But do you think I hang around weird people like that? Look, she doesn't even have hands!" I said incredulously. Finally convinced, they confiscated my passport, looked up my okole, and then released me.

Brent couldn't contain himself when we made $250,000, fifty thousand more than projected. Easy money, at least for him, he threw hundred dollar bills around like a big shot. The quarter mil dwindled to $200,000. I charged the loss to the game. With the balance we opened two auto companies.

Brent opened Preston Motors, an auto wholesale lot in San Diego. I established Botts Enterprises Incorporated, doing business as EuroClassics Auto Rental and Leasing on Maui. Through Preston Motors, we purchased European classics and shipped them to Maui. I sold them under the guise of a fleet reduction. This legally eliminated the red tape and expense of a sales license, and cut my overhead. Aside from the high demand for clean autos in Hawaii, our clientele also included Japanese collectors from Japan.

As planned, we purchased thirty Jeeps from a rental fleet in Hawaii and shipped them to California. Brent had them renovated through a Mexican body shop in San Diego. Once they were repainted, the faded Jeeps looked impressively new. However, my end of the bargain seemed to be getting shortchanged. Brent had a fleet of Jeeps, but stopped sending me cars. To get to the bottom of things, I flew to San Diego.

When I got there, I met Don Kastner and Uncle Nick, Brent's

new assistants. Brent's idea of a hotshot accountant, Uncle Nick was an older, bald, washed up oil rigger from Texas. A bragger with nothing to show, he boasted of having a trove in hidden assets. Kastner in turn, was a total goofball who had a glass eye and noticeable limp from being shot up in Vietnam. According to Brent, Kastner was the best-used car salesman in Southern California.

"This car, that car, they're all going on the docks tomorrow," I said, as I pointed to a half dozen cars parked in his lot.

"But I need the Porsche for a driver, so I can buy cars in L.A.," Brent whined.

"F... you, drive a F...en Toyota. All the Porsches and Beamers are mine. That was the deal," I said furiously. Expecting to see blood, Kastner skipped out the back door. My snap routine worked. A few Porsches and BMWs were immediately shipped off to Hawaii.

In the meantime, I learned more about Kastner. We drove to L.A. from San Diego to sell a Jeep to one of Kastner's connections. He had connections with various auto dealers in Los Angeles, and the bankers that financed those dealerships. A few beers and a Valium later, we arrived. A dorky sales representative came out and carefully examined the sides of the Jeep from the rear.

"What the F... are you looking for? You looking for dents?" Kastner asked aggressively. "The only F...en dent, is right F...en here!" he said, as he pounded his fist on top of the fender. "We've got places to go, people to see, obligations to keep, and nothing's getting done standing around here. So go in and get the F...en check," he said, as he thumped his index finger on the rep's chest.

Within minutes we had the check. I loved Kastner's strategy. He was a radical.

Bitten by greed fever, Brent had to go again. Without my knowledge, he recruited Kastner as a mule. He promised to make him rich. Bad luck worked out for the good. Since my passport had been confiscated, another run wasn't possible. Brent offered to get me a new identity. I continued to remind him that it was a one-time deal, and we shook hands on it. This went on for a year.

Kastner helped with EuroClassics on Maui. I now had a fleet of Porsches and BMWs. In due time, I felt obligated and gave in to Brent's persistence. "O.K., one last time," I said, and laid out my demands to Brent. "A new identity is mandatory, that way if anything goes wrong, I can say that I never left the country. You're paying for everything down to the last drink—plane tickets, hotels, dope, everything. We're going to Chiang Mai together and I'm just going to buy the kilo, that's it. You bring it back to Bangkok, and Kastner carries it back to San Francisco. I have only two conditions. Don't carry a crumb on your bodies and avoid Honolulu Customs like the plague. They're the Gestapo there," I stressed. "And I don't want anybody getting busted, so I want to know how you're bringing it back before we leave."

Through Kastner's connections, I got a new identity. With it, I applied for a passport. Brent purchased the airline tickets. As a cover for his return, Kastner went to the 1988 Summer Olympics. Brent assured me that he a false-bottomed suitcase with him and would meet us in Bangkok with it.

Brent and I flew to Bangkok, and then on to Chiang Mai together. I left him in a hotel, took $10,000 in hundred dollar bills, and visited Charlie in the Karen village. We smoked several bowls of opium before Charlie and two black-cloaked hillbillies led me into the jungles. I gave Charlie the money to purchase the kilo. He scrambled off to meet the chemists. Within minutes of his exit, we met up with two plainclothes Thai drug cops, which was unusual according to the tribesmen. A young American in the middle of nowhere was more peculiar though. We were searched and questioned. Since we didn't have the money or any drugs, they had to let us go. When they left, we quickly got off the trail and blazed through a jungle of ferns and bushes. The hillbillies hid me in a mosquito-infested bush, and then left to meet Charlie.

Mosquitoes hovered like helicopters and attacked like dive-bombers. My only concern was to avoid catching malaria. Minutes turned to hours. For all I knew, Charlie was halfway to Burma and I was lost in the jungles. My malaria phobia subsided. I thought that I got ripped off and left for dead. The only signs of life were the unusual birdcalls echoing through the jungle. Out of desperation, I returned the birdcalls. It was Charlie and the boys calling. They had forgotten which bush I was in.

Charlie had the kilo of heroin. To avoid meeting the cops, we hiked up the side of a mountain. Safely out of harm's way, thousands of feet above the city, we reached a small bamboo hut with a killer view. A fiery orange sunset filled the sky as I smoked the heroin on tin foil. Compressed in a solid white brick, the red "Double Globe" picture stamped on the plastic bag signified its quality and authenticity.

Several hours later, through an obscure jungle of darkness, we stumbled down the mountain to the village. A non-English speaking tribesman packed me out of the village on the back of a motorcycle. I wore a black long sleeve windbreaker and helmet as a disguise. Riding down the long winding road with the kilo of smack under my shirt, I stood ready to toss it at any indication. The biker dropped me off at the bottom of the hill and split. I quickly hailed a taxi and returned to the hotel in Chiang Mai. I met Brent and gave him the kilo. My job was completed. Brent was to meet Kastner in Bangkok. I headed to Pattaya Beach. We would meet there later.

Three days later, Brent and Kastner met me at the Ocean View hotel in Pattaya. Brent told me that he almost got busted at the Chiang Mai airport. The metal detectors buzzed when he went through. The instant camera hanging around his neck set it off. He realized it at the last second when they started to search him. It was another close call. I started to think superstitiously again. Two close calls signified a bad luck streak. He also told me that he left the kilo at the Bangkok Hilton, hidden in his suitcase. This really alarmed me. However, if anybody was going to jail it wasn't going to be me, so I let it ride.

We returned to the Bangkok Hilton a few days later and retrieved their belongings. Our departure was the following day. To ensure that it was fail-safe, I wanted to inspect the false-bottomed suitcase. That's when I found out that Brent didn't have a false-bottomed suitcase. I couldn't believe it.

"Let me get this straight," I started out calmly. "We made an agreement that he was going to carry the dope back in a false-bottomed suitcase right? Now you want him to carry a kilo on his body. Did I miss anything? What's he going to say if he gets caught? 'Duh, I didn't know it was there.' I say we take this kilo and flush it down the toilet right now," I said firmly.

"C'mon," Brent whined, "I've spent over twenty grand already. I think he'll make it."

"Yeah right," I scoffed, "Strike-one—I almost got caught making the pick-up. Then strike-two—you almost got caught bringing it in from Chiang Mai. Now we've got strike-three over here," I said, pointing to Kastner. "Are we going to hit a home run or strike out?" I asked. The bad luck streak was a familiar pattern. I discovered it from banging cars. When things aren't going right, stop whatever you're doing. The warning was loud and clear to me.

"Don't do it Kastner. You won't make it. Why take a chance. We can always do it again another time," I said. Kastner believed me, but wasn't sure.

"Don't listen to Botts, he's just a snappo," Brent said. "I say just load it up and we roll a hard eight. I think you'll make it."

Kastner bought Brent's argument. I was exasperated. I know when I'm right, but knew they wouldn't listen to me anyway. I gave up and shook my head. "F... it, you guys are on your own," I said. "Good luck Don, 'cause you're going to need it."

I gave Kastner a hug the next morning before leaving the hotel. I knew he was a goner. We boarded different flights and I never saw him again. Brent screwed up on his ticket also. Kastner was booked on a flight to San Francisco via Honolulu. He met up with the Gestapo and was busted on the spot.

Brent and I breezed through Customs in San Francisco, and then waited at his house in San Diego. I thought Kastner pulled a fast one when we didn't hear from him. A few days later, Kastner's roommate called and informed us of his arrest in Honolulu. I didn't believe him. Nobody could be that stupid. When reality set in, I felt winded. It was too late to argue.

"Don't listen to Botts, he's just a snappo," I told Brent, mimicking his famous last words. "We belong in jail right now, not Kastner."

Brent nodded his head silently. I couldn't blame him though. I knew he'd get greedy. I also knew that Kastner wouldn't make it, but despite my instincts I let them persuade me otherwise. This taught me to trust in God and my intuition, regardless of who says I'm wrong and in my heart I know otherwise.

As a liaison, my attorney visited Kastner at Halawa jail. My main concern was his solidarity. According to our calculations of the post-1987 Federal Sentencing Guidelines, Kastner was facing a sentence of eight to ten years without parole. The only way a judge could depart from the guidelines was when a defendant co-operated with the government. To keep him pacified, I sent his mother $1000 a month.

CHAPTER SIX

ULUWATU, BALI

"Life doesn't get much better!" exclaimed my stunning young blond friend in her skimpy black string-bikini. I couldn't have agreed with her more. Illuminated from the Hawaiian sunshine, the ocean was a clear deep blue. A school of Dolphins guided our boat around the southern tip of Lanai Island. Soaking up the rays and drinking cold beers, it was another day in paradise.

The jackpot was lining up. A year had passed since Kastner's arrest, and EuroClassics was prospering. That's when I met Wayne. Like me, Wayne was a thirty-two year old bartender at a crossroads in life. His wife divorced him and took his two kids. Then his father died and left him an inheritance. Attracted to the glamour of my lifestyle, Wayne invested part of his inheritance in EuroClassics and became Secretary/Treasurer of my corporation.

I ran into Derek at a Billabong surf contest on Oahu. Ranked #1 on the pro surf circuit, he was competing in the Billabong. We were old friends from Waimanalo. After the contest, he was going to Bali. It had always been my fantasy to surf Uluwatu in Bali. I needed a break and it was a perfect chance. I decided to meet him there.

Wayne oversaw EuroClassics while I flew to Bali via Los Angeles. Combining business with pleasure, I inspected a Porsche 911 at a dealership in Newport Beach. The white cabriolet with black top and tan interior was a perfect convertible for Maui. I bought it on the spot and shipped it to Hawaii. To kill a few days, I visited Brent in San Diego.

Uncle Nick was back working at Preston Motors. Brent had supposedly fired him for embezzling, but for some reason he had re-hired him. Upon hearing of my trip to Bali, Uncle Nick approached me with a scheme to meet him in Thailand. He wanted to mule back a load of heroin. His timing couldn't have been better. I decided to meet him in Bangkok on my return from Bali. I also agreed to pay his way, so I called Wayne on Maui. Without giving any particulars, I asked Wayne to purchase Nick a round-trip ticket to Bangkok and give him a few grand. The following day I flew to Bali via Singapore.

Drunk and jet-lagged, I arrived in Singapore at 3:00 a.m. The following morning I bought a Rolex, drank a Singapore Sling at the Raffles Hotel, and then continued on to Bali. Custom agents immediately cleared me through Denpasar Airport. I was just another surfer visiting Bali. At the airport, I reserved an ocean front cottage on Kuta Beach and rented a Jeep for the week.

Kuta Beach is a long white beach set amongst a tropical setting of coconut, banana and papaya trees. I could've gone to Kauai without knowing the difference. Settled into a cozy ocean front cottage, the sound of surf and thunder from a distant storm lulled me to sleep. I drove to Uluwatu the following morning with my surfboard. The rainforest was reminiscent of old Hawaii. The roads were bumpy and most of the vehicles were Jeeps. On the way, I passed Balinese children on the road. They resembled Hawaiians, and spoke Hawaiian Pidgin English. "Howzit brah, hang loose mongoose," they shouted when they recognized me as a surfer, slang used by Hawaiian surfers.

When I reached Uluwatu, a young Balinese boy packed me down a long narrow trail on a Honda. A large concession stand sat atop rocky cliffs that overlooked the ocean. It had a panoramic view of the cliffs and expanse. It was the time of year that the swells rolled in, but the ocean was calm. I knew that it was just a matter of time. In the meantime, I enjoyed the serenity with a cup of hot tea, and let my mind drift away with the scenery.

The following morning I returned at sunrise with my Nikon camera. When I arrived, I heard the crisp sound of a tube crackling in. Excited by the familiar sound, I ran down to the jagged rocks in time to see a perfect five-foot wave barreling in. It was a freak wave, known as a rogue wave, and I didn't see another one like it again.

Derek arrived that afternoon with a few pro surfers from Hawaii. The surf was almost flat, but we were anxious to "get wet." We paddled out into two-foot ankle snappers. By evening, the surf diminished when the tide went out. I focused my concentration on the horizon. There appeared to be lines across the horizon. I remembered the rogue wave in the morning. I had an excited feeling inside. I knew that a swell was about to hit.

We had lobsters and beer together that evening. I tried to convince them that the following day was going to be the "BIG DAY." I must've sounded like an idiot. They were the best surfers in the world. It seemed impossible; the surf couldn't get that big overnight. Yet it was simple math to me. They ignored my prediction. Instead, they wanted to play with the monkeys in the jungle. I knew otherwise, and returned to Uluwatu at the crack of dawn.

A surprise fifteen-foot swell rolled in overnight. I was one of the few to catch dawn patrol. It was a surfer's fantasy. I surfed until the wind picked up, and then returned to my cottage. The surf pounded Kuta Beach as I ate breakfast. I couldn't contain my excitement. The swell seemed to be getting bigger, so I sped back to Uluwatu for another session. Derek and the boys arrived by then.

"How were the monkeys?" I teased Derek, rubbing it in for not listening to my prediction. He didn't answer.

The waves wrapped around a massive coral reef shelf. We paddled out through the channel. It was insane. Sets were averaging fifteen feet. By 4:00 that afternoon, the wind died down and the tide went out. The conditions were perfect. Huge glassy tubes broke over the shallow inside reef.

The intensity of challenging nature inside of a tube is the ultimate natural high, but treacherous if you wipe-out. It was through surfing that I cultured an extremist attitude. "Charge 'em" was our motto. Quitting isn't an option. Derek and I were the last ones out, striving for one last good wave before sunset. A gigantic set caught me inside. Derek barely made it through each wave in time. Six monstrous waves pounded me one after the other. I felt like a cat in a washing machine. I didn't know which way was up. Using my surf-leash, I found my way to the surface through a sea of foam. My lungs craved air. I thought the worst was over when I surfaced. In-between burps of foam and gasps for air, I looked up at the next avalanche of water cascading upon me. I thought I was going to drown. *Help me Jesus* was my only hope. Winded to the max, my ribcage was bruised from a massive overdose of hyperventilating. I just laid on my board and drifted in afterwards.

"Hey Andy, did you get caught by that last set?" Derek asked after catching his last wave in, knowing that I did.

"Yeah," I moaned. He erupted in laughter. "F... you," I managed to chuckle. I knew that it was his turn to rub it in.

The swell remained strong for a few days. I was dying for a joint. Indonesia is a serious non-drug country, so I didn't bring any pakalolo with me. Smuggling or possessing illegal drugs is punishable by death. Thailand had serious drug laws as well, but was lax on marijuana. I had a few weeks to kill before Uncle Nick's arrival, so I continued on to Bangkok, Thailand.

I caught a taxi directly to Pattaya Beach and picked up the first escort who could score a bag of ganja. My first joint in a week, wham, bam, I rolled over and passed out. Pattaya was always a fun town, but the novelty wore off. Hungry for a new adventure, I booked a day tour to the gem factories in Chantaburi. A few older European couples booked the same tour. We piled into a Toyota van driven by an English speaking Thai guide. It reminded me of a family tour.

I was amazed at how much Thailand still had to offer. In route, we passed a crocodile farm, golf course, and Thai Grand Prix racetrack. Our guide navigated a detour off-road through the sapphire mines. It looked like the moon after a meteor shower. Twenty-foot deep Volkswagen-sized pits were spread out every fifteen feet. Using Flintstone-type machinery, mud-bathed peasants manually cranked up buckets of mud from the pits. The mud was poured onto a water wheel that separated the sapphires from the sludge. Off to the side, a fat, older Thai lady with rotten teeth smiled and held out her hands. In them was a selection of polished colored stones. I bought a star sapphire for five bucks. My guide considered it a rip-off. He advised me to wait until we reached the ruby factory. We piled back into the van and our family tour continued. Several miles later, we arrived at a two-story cement building that could've passed for a bomb shelter.

Skeptically, I entered what I expected to be another tourist trap. Behind glass panes on the bottom floor, underpaid Thais worked tirelessly, cutting, polishing and setting red stones into rings, pendants and broaches. We were led upstairs to meet the ruby broker. He didn't say a word. Instead, he poured a bag of shiny red rocks onto the table. Rubies of every shade, size and shape glistened brilliantly. Almost immediately, he scooped the stones back up and poured out a bag of larger stones. He did this five times. Priced according to karat, not quality, prices were set at a fraction of U.S. retail.

"The pidgin blood rubies are best," my guide informed me as I picked up a dime-sized ruby and held it to the light.

"What color is a pidgin's blood?" I asked.

"This one," he said expertly, pointing to a five-karat, deep red, heart-shaped ruby. For 2000 baht ($80.00 U.S.), I bought what looked to me like the crown jewel.

After we returned to Pattaya, I found another jewel; my new girlfriend for the week. With a week left to kill before Uncle Nick's arrival, we caught a plane to Phuket Island. Phuket is a resort set amongst a collection of lush, green, islands scattered in the Gulf of Thailand. In a class by itself, the brothel, go-go bar, and red-light nightlife are non-existent. A get-away spot for the wealthy, exclusive beach resorts stretch the coastline. Nearby islands can be reached by Jet Ski, but I chose to rent a motorcycle. My girlfriend beat on my back as I blazed around the coastal roads on a Yamaha. In the prime of my life, I couldn't have felt better.

On the eve of Uncle Nick's arrival, we flew back to Bangkok and rented a room at the Airport Hotel. To surprise him, I picked up a Thai girl who gave great massages. At midnight, I crossed the overpass connecting the hotel with Don Muang airport, formerly known as Bangkok International. The girls waited in my hotel room. For two hours, I watched every passenger exit from Customs, including the flight crew. Nick was a no-show. I returned to my room and called Wayne on Maui.

"No, he made the flight, I put him on myself," Wayne said. "But you know what, something seemed strange about him. Are you sure about him?" he asked.

"Nah, don't worry, he's Brent's uncle. Maybe I just missed him coming out," I assured him.

At 3:30 a.m., I finally got a call from Uncle Nick. Within a few minutes we met in my room. "So do you think we can get two kilos with this?" he asked anxiously, handing me the $4000 that Wayne had given him.

"Two kilos," I scoffed, "Two ounces maybe. Aside from that, I'm out of spending money. In the meantime, you can take a hot shower if you want," I said, as it's usually the first thing that I want after a long flight.

"No, that's all right. I'll take one later," he said.

"Whatever," I said, and then introduced the girl that I picked up for him. "This is Nook. She gives great massages. I got her for you," I said, pointing to Nook and motioning her over to Nick.

"NO! Don't touch me," he blurted out, backing away from her advance, "Later on."

I wondered if he was gay or something. Even Nook had a puzzled look on her face. This was Brent's Uncle Nick though, so I let it ride. Just in case, I left Nook behind with Uncle Nick, and then checked into another hotel with my girlfriend.

For the next few days, my taxi driver chauffeured us around Bangkok. I kept him as my personal driver because he spoke English and scored pakalolo for me. Our flight home was scheduled for July 10, five days away. After ordering a few tailor-fitted suits, I flew off to Chiang Mai. Uncle Nick stayed behind with my taxi driver.

The dirt trail leading to the Karen village became a sea of mud. It was rainy season. My Yamaha motorcycle trudged through the sludge. For a few bucks, a Toyota truck with snow chains drove me the remaining few miles into the village. I met Charlie in the village. A regular customer now, after a few bowls of opium, I purchased four ounces of China White heroin. With the dope in my crotch, I rode out of the hills and returned to Chiang Mai.

I couldn't remember the way back to my hotel. Every street

looked the same. Amongst a row of condemnable buildings, a "Hard Rock Café" sign stood out. I stopped for directions. It was a rundown bar that infringed on the franchise's logo. Two Thai girls smiled and giggled when I walked in and straddled up to the bar. "Somesing drink sir?" one of the girls asked.

After a few Gin and tonics, I picked up a Hard Rock-Chiang Mai T-shirt and a bargirl as souvenirs. She pronounced Hard Rock as Hard Luck Café. I found it ironic. Her blue jeans and tight T-shirt revealed a body found on models. On the back of my bike, she directed me back to my hotel and stayed with me for the next few days.

That evening, we dined out on the town. I had an elaborate Chinese meal of Tiger prawns, sweet sour pork and chicken fried rice. My new girlfriend preferred Thai delicacies: spicy kidneys, liver soup and an assortment of indigestible dishes. Three days later, I flew back to Bangkok with the dope in a false-bottomed shaving cream can. Hoping to see her again, I left my business card with her.

My taxi driver faithfully awaited my return at Don Muang airport. However, I couldn't recall informing him of the day and time of my arrival. Experiencing short-term memory loss from my heroin-induced fog, I assumed that Uncle Nick had told him, although I wasn't sure if I had told him either. "Good afternoon Mr. Andrew. How are you?" he asked.

"Fine, fine, how's everything with you?" I said.

In route to my hotel, we stopped at the tailor's shop to pick-up my new suits. "I think you being followed," my driver said after we left.

"Who? How do you know?" I asked.

"I don't know, I think is American man," he said, looking in his rear view mirror. I thought he was pulling my leg.

"Can you lose him?" I asked to be sure.

"I'll try," he said, and then stepped on the accelerator. He weaved through Bangkok rush-hour traffic. I expected a collision.

"Did you lose him?" I asked when we reached my hotel.

"I think so," he said, still looking around as he got my bags from the trunk. He then carried them to my room.

"You bring dope with you?" he asked, after we entered my room. "If you have, flush toilet now."

Taxi drivers are famous for turning in foreigners. I thought he had figured out why I went to Chiang Mai, and was trying to finger me. "No. Why?" I asked cautiously.

"You sure?" he persisted, "If you have, flush toilet now."

It seemed peculiar. I contemplated flushing the heroin down the toilet, but it was worth $80,000. I didn't want to jump the gun. Instead, I flushed a bag of ganja that I bought from him. I considered flushing the stash later, but when I warned Uncle Nick, he wasn't alarmed. He still wanted to carry it back to San Francisco. Reluctantly, I gave him the heroin-filled can the night before our departure.

We got off to an early start for our 2:00 p.m. flight to San Francisco. I injected a large dose of heroin while Nick packed the suitcases. What was just another departure from the "Land of Smiles," we crawled through the smog-infested traffic. We arrived at Don Muang airport three hours early. As a tip, I gave the remainder of my Thai currency to the taxi driver. At the check-in counter, I gave my credit card to the counter agent for the departure tax.

"So solly sir, only cash," he said, pointing to a small 'No credit cards accepted' sign posted on the check-in counter.

"Can I leave our bags?" I asked, "I'll go over to the airport bank, I'll be right back."

"Yes, no ploblem," he said with a smile.

I couldn't get any cash from the airport bank or the Visa machines. The computers just happened to be down. I'd never heard of an ATM machine going on the blink, but this was Bangkok. Nobody knew how long they would be down either. My only option was to catch a cab back to Bangkok. I left Uncle Nick at the check-in counter and dashed outside to the curb. A cab took me back to Bangkok, where we found a bank that would honor my credit card.

When I returned with the cash, the counter was closed. Uncle Nick stood off to the side with our luggage. Exasperated, I swore at Nick for retrieving the bags. In turn, he blamed the clerk at the counter.

"So solly sir, you have to go counter six," the clerk informed us, as he pointed across the lobby.

We still had time. I hurried across the lobby with my Nikon camera slung around my neck and suitcase in tow. Out of nowhere, eight Thais swooped upon me. Four of them had cameras. The others wore tan colored jumpsuits. I was surrounded. If I was anyone else, I would've thought they were the paparazzi.

"Just a moment sir; we are drug police. You look suspicious," proposed a short Thai with thin mustache and beady eyes, dressed in a tan jumpsuit, who appeared to be the ringleader.

"What do you mean suspicious?" I protested, "I've got a plane to catch."

"No," he insisted, "I think you better wait. We like to check you."

"O.K., go ahead and look," I said, and handed him my suitcase and camera. From the corner of my eye, twenty feet away, I spotted Uncle Nick. To keep them from linking us, I avoided eye contact.

"No, not here," instructed the ringleader, "Please come with us," he said, and then led me into a small room off to the side.

Once inside, the ringleader pulled out my toiletry bag, opened it up, and produced the shaving cream can that I gave to Uncle Nick. "This is yours?" he asked, accusingly.

I was stunned. Experiencing major memory loss from my intoxication, unanswered questions swirled in my mind. I couldn't remember if or when I gave the can to Nick, or if he accidentally packed it in my bag. "No, that's not mine. I think the taxi driver put it there," I lied spontaneously.

They proceeded to roll it on the ground to see if it wobbled or rolled. An old trick to test false cans, wobbling indicates fluid. The can raced smoothly across the floor. I knew that I was doomed. Not realizing that the can simply unscrewed open, they broke open the bottom of the can with a hammer and screwdriver. A bag of CW heroin protruded from the bottom. I was instantly handcuffed and the can of dope was placed in my hands. I put my head down as the photo shoot began. I'd be on the front page of the *Bangkok Post*.

The ringleader found half of a business card in my wallet. The other half was used as a crutch to hold my last joint. "Aha," he exclaimed. "This half you keep until delivery. Your contact has other half. You match together," he said shrewdly. *Great deduction Watson*, I didn't even try to explain. I just shrugged my shoulders in submission while they did a field test.

They placed the bag of dope on a scale. It weighed 114 grams. A small scoop of dope was mixed in a small hard plastic vile of fluid. The vile was then crushed to bring out a color. The fluid turned purple, the shade for 90–98% pure heroin. "Number four, Number four," they shouted victoriously (Number four is the highest grade).

"You want talk to American police?" the ringleader asked.

"The DEA?" I asked. "No thanks, that's quite alright."

"No, I think you better," he insisted.

Here we go again, I thought to myself, knowing I had no say in the matter. I knew that I was in deep kukai. I just didn't know how deep. "What kind of punishment am I facing?" I asked him.

"Exporting over one hundred grams of heroin is punishable by gunshot to the head until dead," he said seriously.

I was shell-shocked. *So this is how it all ends*, I thought. He could see the far-away look in my eyes.

"Don't worry, I think you lucky, maybe you only get life," he said, as if that was any consolation.

"How's that," I asked. He explained that I'd be charged for the actual pure weight after a laboratory analysis. If I was lucky, the actual weight could be less than a hundred grams. I'd then get life instead of death.

Lucky, I thought. *Why am I always told that I'm lucky when I look death in the eyes?* I flipped a car when I was nineteen years old, and crushed my mid-spine. I was put into traction, hospitalized for a month, and given morphine injections every four hours. The nurses remarked that I was "Incredibly lucky." The X-rays showed the fracture a hairline away from my spinal cord. I should've been paralyzed at the least. If it touched my spinal cord, I would've been in a wheel chair for life. *Luck, shmuck, my friends were lucky*, was the way I saw it. They didn't get hurt at all. Now I'm facing the firing squad, and I'm "Lucky."

A stocky Hawaiian-Filipino DEA agent entered the backroom. "Hi, I'm Rudy; they tell me you ran into a little problem here." he said congenially. "I'm from Maui, where are you from?"

"Really, so am I," I said, and proceeded to give him the same B.S. taxi driver story.

A tall, slim haole with short, wavy blond hair entered the room. "F... you and your taxi driver story," he shouted. "I've been following your ass all over Chiang Mai for the past three days," he said, and plopped down a photo that I gave to a cocktail waitress in Chiang Mai. "My job is to put people like you away," he said, furious. "We've got hundreds of hours of phone taps on you Mr. Botts," he said, as he pointed his finger at me. "Do you know Donald Kastner?" he asked.

I was stunned again. I tried to figure out how they picked-up on me. I've always been cautious when using the telephone and it wasn't a crime to know somebody. "Yeah, I know Kastner, so what?" I said, hoping to glean info from him.

"Did you buy the kilo for him?" he asked.

"I didn't leave the country," I said, my pre-planned alibi in the Kastner case.

"That's not what I asked you," he said, furious.

"I'm sorry. I'm facing either life or death and can't even think right now," I said passively.

"Well think long and hard then," he said, and shoved six blank pieces of paper in my hand. "The next time we talk to you, we want these filled up front and back. We have a file on you since 1977. We want to know about every trip you've made, exactly what you did, how much dope you bought, and who you sold it to," he demanded.

This guy is crazy, I thought. *They'd definitely execute me if I confessed to all of that.*

"Do you like fried rice?" he asked.

"Yeah," I said. "Why?" I asked confused. I completely missed the point, if there was a point. Fried rice is a delicacy in Hawaii.

"Because you're going to have a lot of it," he said. "Throw him to the dogs," he told the Thais.

As I was led out the door, Rudy sang "Aloha Oe," the infamous song that Queen Liliuokolani wrote when she lost the Kingdom of Hawaii.

CHAPTER SEVEN

BANGKOK HILTON

Wedged between two Thai Narks, in the backseat of a Toyota police car, I stared at the gloomy thunderclouds that closed in on us. Depression besieged me as they sped to the police station; sirens bleeping. My life was over. Turned over to the cops at Don Muang Police Station, before being locked in a cell, they allowed me to pick-out clothes from my suitcase. I changed into my swim shorts and Aloha shirt. To evade another jones, I feigned a cough so I could get the methadone in my toiletry bag. It resembled cough syrup in its little plastic container. Given to me without a second thought, I downed it before they realized what it was.

I was then locked into one of three, fifteen by fifteen-foot cells. The men were confined to the two on the left—the women in the cell on the right. All of the cells were left open during the day. For a fee, the day-shift cops ran out to the street vendors and bought food. The night-shift cops brought ganja and Mekong whiskey. Money talked, everything was for sale.

Up to eight cellmates were laid out on a hardwood floor. In the corner, a four-foot high wall, three feet wide, surrounded a porcelain hole-in-the-ground. Next to this squat toilet, a small cement trough was filled with water. To rinse or shower, we used a rusted coffee can to scoop water from the trough.

I was abruptly awoken the first morning. It sounded like a riot had broken out on the streets. I thought it was another coup de tat. I climbed atop the cement wall of our bathroom and peered through the hollow cement tiles that served as a window. A parade of Thais clanged pans, banged on makeshift drums, and chanted a horrid tune. As they passed by, they jumped and danced in the street as if they were on LSD. At home they would've been arrested for insanity. I realized that it was normal when they danced by the police station the following morning.

I spent the next five days with an assortment of misfits being held for minor offenses. A younger Thai told me about "Bumbut Pisset Two" (Bumbut). He told me that I'd be transferred there after leaving the police station. I couldn't imagine how much harsher it could get, but it sounded bleak. He tried to convince me that suicide was a better alternative. "It's better to die young. For a better life next time," he explained, according to his warped interpretation of Buddhism. I decided to watch the movie a little longer.

Three dark skinned, Sri Lankan "Freedom fighters," were being held for expired visas. Terrorists for all I knew, they had Bin Laden style beards, prayed towards Mecca four times a day, and refused to eat anything containing pork. The tallest one collapsed whenever he paced the cell. He had a bullet hole through his leg the size of a silver dollar. I was astounded, yet it didn't faze his partners. It was an everyday thing to them.

A Thai junkie came in for shoplifting a pack of cigarettes. He immediately scrounged a smoke from one of the Freedom Fighters, and then crouched below eye level in the squat toilet area. It turned out that he had four ounces of heroin and was filling the cigarette with heroin—called a choker. Five minutes later, the cops called him out for his interrogation and noticed how stoned he was. They frisked him and found the stash in his underwear. He now faced real time, but was too stoned to care. He returned to the cell and passed out on the floor. The following morning he woke up sick as a dog.

An American Embassy representative, who was probably DEA, visited me the day after my arrest. He retrieved my suitcase, and gave me a list of Thai lawyers and their phone numbers. The Thai cops let me call an attorney that I chose from the list. It was the last time that I used a phone for a while.

I expected to be formerly charged when I was transported to court on the fifth day. Handcuffed to one of my Thai cellmates, in the back of a canvas covered Toyota truck, a Thai cop sleepily guarded the exit of the truck. It was a perfect opportunity to escape, but the prospect was futile this time. I was broke, alone and ten thousand miles from home.

We arrived at a Municipal-type building. Thai writing marked the entrance. I assumed it was the courthouse. Led into the building, amidst a crowd of rubbernecking Asians, I felt like I was lost in a weird dream. At the entrance, a Thai dressed in a cheap suit introduced himself as the lawyer whom I contacted at the police station. We talked briefly as they led me through the crowded building. I was shuttled into a wooden-partitioned room. The lawyer wasn't allowed inside. It was a makeshift courtroom. Seated on a backless wooden bench, I was given what looked like the official charges, written in Thai. The hearing was also spoken in Thai. I found out that it was a formality to prolong the investigation for twelve more days. This continuation could also be extended seven times, meaning that I could be held for up to three months without charges. Unable to read the allegations, I gave the Arabic-type document to my lawyer as I was led away. He promised to visit the following week.

Taken downstairs, I entered a corridor. Cells were crammed with prisoners to my right. Arms dangled through the bars as I passed. A wire-meshed screen to my left covered the bars that faced the street. Families shouted through the bars from the street. Prisoner's hollered back. The chatter was deafening. I then passed two lines of Thais dressed in bright orange potato bags. They squatted in unison with thick elephant chains welded to their ankles. I expected to be chained and clothed like them throughout my incarceration. They quickly chirped off in sequence, "Noong, song, sam, see, ha, hoke, jet, bat, cow..." I thought it was roll call. I later learned that they were counting off in Thai.

Through a large iron gate, I was ushered into a piss-stench cell littered with cigarette butts. A hundred Thai junkies were lying on the ground and puking everywhere. Those with strength fiendishly smoked hand-rolled cigarettes. Nicotine stained their fingers. The guard opened the gate and tossed in a package of food. Ten Thais devoured it in a minute. I sat in the corner and watched. The gate opened again. A huge guard stood at the entrance. He was furious for some reason. The scrawny Thai sleeping near the gate got three swift kicks to the head with black steel-toed boots. I couldn't believe my eyes. Fearing that I'd be the next, I stayed away from the gate. The only person who could speak English was a Thai with deep heroin tracks a foot long down each arm. "What your nationality?" he asked me.

I thought for a moment before answering. *Let's see, my mother's French, my father's German-English-Irish, but I'm from Hawaii.*

"Are you American?" he asked before I could answer.

"Huh, yeah I guess so," I said. "Where'd you learn your English?" I asked.

"I stay Bangkwang prison fifteen years. Last year go home. American man teach me English," he said.

"Fifteen years! That's a long time. Is that how you got those tracks?" I asked, pointing to the wounds on his arms.

"Yes, I use heloin the whole time," he said.

I couldn't imagine how anybody could be strung-out on heroin for such a long time, especially in prison. Yet his tracks were real, giving me a glimpse of what my life could soon be like. He also told me about the executions carried out at Bangkwang Prison—the condemned are held on death row for several years with elephant chains welded to their ankles. Covered with a sheet and chained to a cross, prisoners are shot to death by a mounted machine gun. The following morning he's taken down from the blood stained cross, and his family can have what's left of the body.

After a long, boring day without any food, the setting sun darkened my dreary cell. A dispiriting feeling overcame me.

The moment I dreaded came. I was transported to Bumbut. The guards, dressed in tan-colored uniforms, crammed the hundred Thai junkies into an enclosed wire-meshed paddy wagon. I was jammed in last with an Arab. The gate was firmly slammed behind us. I squeezed down to the floor, and sat with my knees crammed into my face. An acerbic smell protruded from the Thai junkies. It was heroin sweat. The stench, lack of air, and humidity turned the wagon into a foul smelling sauna. The driver sped through heavy traffic. Every few minutes he braked abruptly. I became wedged between the grimy Thais and the wire gate. Three drunken guards guarded the rear. A machine gun was aimed directly at me. The smallest of the three guards was an older, balding Thai, who waved his machine gun around carelessly and shouted commands in Thai. The Thai junkies cringed in silence. His partner hung out of the bus as if trying to catch streetlights. The third guard hung onto him in a drunken stupor.

After an hour of bobbing and weaving through traffic, we arrived at a fortress of thick cement walls over twenty feet high. Manned gun towers dotted the perimeter. We drove through a pair of solid iron gates. Once inside, we were let out. It was a reprieve to be separated from the stench-ridden Thais. Signs written in Thai were posted on the walls. Only one was in English. "Bumbut Pisset Two, Thailand's Medical Center for Drug Addicted Offenders," it read. I stood next to the Arab, the only other foreigner. The Thais quickly squatted again. "Noong, song, sam, see, ha, hoke, jet, bat, cow, sip...."

Prepared for the worst, we were led through a corridor of tall walls. Nature scenes were skillfully hand-painted on the walls.

It was a temporary distraction from the horrors within. We entered the prison and lined-up for a strip search. Four Blue-shirts seemed to be in charge. Blue-shirts were inmate trustees dressed in Boy Scout uniforms. They did everything a guard was supposed to do; searches, mail, visits, etc. The Blue-shirts addressed the guards as Commodores and bowed. I thought they were kissing ass, until I learned that Commodore was the name for guard. To prevent a prisoner from impersonating a Commodore, long pants and jewelry were prohibited. My Rolex was promptly confiscated. Blue jeans were cut down to shorts. A Blue-shirt then collected the court papers.

"What your case?" he demanded, after I told him that I had given mine to my lawyer.

"Heroin," I replied.

"How much?" he said, irritated.

"About a hundred grams," I said, rounding off the weight.

"More or less than a hundred?" he asked quickly.

"Less than a hundred," I lied, which saved me from wearing ten-kilo elephant chains for my first three months.

Everybody busted with over a hundred grams wears chains. Chains are heavy iron links looped through thick iron hooks. The hooks encircle each ankle, and then are hammered shut with a sledgehammer. Changing pants with chains on is complicated. It costs two packs of cigarettes to learn the trick.

I was starving. I asked the Commodore who stole my Rolex if I could buy something to eat. He laughed. I assumed there was a language barrier. "Food, food. You know, eat, eat?" I repeated, pointing to my mouth and stomach in a broken English pantomime. He laughed harder. On my third attempt, he erupted uncontrollably in laughter, bringing tears to his eyes. It also brought tears to mine. I realized that I wasn't going to be fed.

After this orientation, I followed the gang of Thais down a long cement road wide enough for trucks. Ten cement buildings lined the road on both sides. Room lights silhouetted the iron-meshed windows on the second floors. The bottom floors were darkened. Well-manicured hedges bordered the perimeters of the buildings. Chest-high gates protruded through the hedges. Led through the gates, we entered Building three.

Two large steel pots sat in the middle of a long picnic table, the length of the bottom floor. I was given my first plate of food. It literally smelled like discarded pig's slop. A ration of purplish, red colored rice was dished out from one pot, and a dark, mushroom looking mixture from the other. I couldn't tell what it was, but I could've sworn it was still moving. My hunger pains told my instinct to survive that I'd better get used to it. I held my nose, gobbled down a few bites, immediately washed it down with tap water, and had diarrhea for the next few days.

After dinner, we took a birdbath from a long water trough. A Blue-shirt lent me a bar of soap and a plastic bowl. My first bath was cold water scooped out bowl by bowl from the trough. I dried off with my t-shirt. Afterwards, I followed the gang upstairs, and waited outside of a caged room. In another caged room, across the hall, were two other Americans; Waterbed and Captain Krunch.

"Welcome to the Bangkok Hilton. Where you from?" shouted Waterbed, a burly Californian with short-cropped hair.

"I'm from Hawaii," I shouted back.

"What the hell you doing here?" he asked.

"Not visiting, that's for sure."

"What'd they bust you for?"

"Smack," I said, grimly.

"Airport?" he asked.

"Yep."

"Ha! Another f...en airport case," he said. "They've been nailing a lot of guys there lately."

"Great, now you tell me," I said, and then entered room nine with the hundred Thais and Arab that I came in with.

Room nine was a fifteen by thirty-foot room. A narrow strip of floor separated the long wooden planks set two-feet above the floor. The Thais were laid out like Sardines. Head to toe, toe to head. No mats or blankets were provided. The Arab slept on the floor near the squat toilet at the head of the room, simply because he was a middle easterner. I was given a mat in the corner, comfortable in comparison, because I was an American. Americans represented power. We saved them from Communism. All westerners were considered Kayais, because they had money. Money represented power. A Kayai is someone considered important; i.e. politician, cop, businessman, or a reputable criminal. Basically, if you had money, you were a Kayai. If not, you suck. Most of the Thais were treated as dogs. If they sat up or talked, they were hit with thin bamboo sticks on their heads and backs.

I awoke abruptly at 2:00 a.m. My stomach gurgled in pain from the slop I had washed down earlier. I felt the gas ready to explode. I'm glad I didn't mistake it for a fart. Tiptoeing over heads, stepping on a few feet and hands, I carefully yet hurriedly made my way to the squat toilet at the opposite end of the room. With barely a moment to spare, my bowels exploded diarrhea full force. If the sound didn't awaken the room, the smell did.

Captain Krunch fetched me the following morning, and fed me real food until I got situated. Krunch was a tall, skinny Brooklyn Jew. He was a sailor. His gang nicknamed him Captain Krunch because he broke everything that he touched. Krunch was sentenced to fifteen years for ganja; the maximum for Pot. He got busted with two tons. According to Thai law, his sentence would've been cut in half if he pled guilty.

Waterbed was also a major ganja smuggler who fought his case, lost, and was sentenced to the max. They paid a bribe to serve their sentences at Bumbut. Sentences of over a year were usually served at Klong Prem. Mr. Somchai was their intermediary and protection. He was a Thai politician whose ganja farms were shut down by the military. During the day, they lived under a lean-to with a rusted iron roof, set between the stairs and divider wall of Building three.

As I exited the steel caged staircase, my first glimpse focused on the shed of squat toilets. Ten Thais squatted side by side in small stalls. One hand held onto the rail of a short cement wall. The other reached behind their shoulder. They resembled greyhounds at the starting gate of a dog race. To the left, the water trough shower ran parallel to the squat toilets. A twenty-foot high wall topped with rusted barbed wire ran the length of the section. It separated Bumbut from Klong Prem Prison. Klong Prem held prisoners with sentences under thirty years, while Bumbut was a pre-trial facility. Sentences over thirty years, including life and death, were confined at Bangkwang Prison.

Captain Krunch told me about the dos and don'ts while imprisoned in Thailand, and emphasized his distrust for the American Embassy. "Don't believe a word they say, they're all liars, and the embassy rep who visits every month works for the DEA. Don't trust her," he said decisively. He also lent me his copy of "A Handbook for Americans Imprisoned in Thailand," by Attorney Dick Atkins, legal counsel for International Recoveries, based in Philadelphia, Pennsylvania.

Atkins has been active in negotiating American Transfer Treaties since 1977, when the first treaty went into effect with Mexico. He was also directly involved in negotiating a treaty with the Thai government, and has testified before the Senate Foreign Relations Committee on international transfer agreements. The Thai government was strongly opposed to a treaty, which began over ten years prior to my arrest. They initially agreed to a prisoner's transfer after they served a minimum of eight years. A lot of prisoners had died by then. As a compromise, the U.S. Congress included a provision that exempted anyone convicted with more than a kilo from transferring. The Thais eventually agreed to the provisions, and a treaty was ratified. However, nobody had actually transferred on this treaty.

Waterbed and Captain Krunch played badminton while I read the handbook. It was a daily routine to release their aggression. Waterbed was a huge Californian. Within an hour, a bed of sweat dripped onto the badminton court; Waterbed. Captain Krunch swung his racket clumsily. Everybody kept their distance when Krunch was on the court.

"That was in," Waterbed shouted, after another birdie landed outside.

"That was out by a mile," Krunch yelled back.

"Bullshit! How would you know you colorblind idiot?"

"Just because I'm colorblind doesn't mean I can't see," Krunch argued, as they faced off between the net.

"Come here you little bastard. Put your neck between my hands so I can choke you," Waterbed said, joking.

I was kept amused as I browsed through the handbook. According to the provisions in the treaty, if I received a sentence that was less than life, I would be eligible to transfer back to an American federal prison after four years. With a life sentence, I'd have to serve eight years until I was eligible. Upon returning to the U.S., all treaty cases are reviewed by the U.S. Parole Commission. A prisoner's release is determined according to the post-1987 guidelines, applicable in my case, or the pre-1987 parole guidelines for those arrested before November 1987. The release guidelines are determined according to the weight and type of drugs convicted for in the foreign country, and applied according to U.S. law.

I realized that I didn't have a fighting chance in a Thai court. I'd also sound silly if I went into court and told the truth. Everyone claims that they were set-up. I also knew that I'd get life instead of death if the weight of the drugs fell below a hundred grams. I now learned that it would be reduced again if I pled guilty. Even if I got fifty years, I could transfer home after four years. I just had to hope that someone would be transferred in the next five years. I saw it as an act of faith. The prison doors had opened before and would open again.

Krunch wasn't as optimistic. "It'll never happen. They've been talking about this treaty for ten years, and they're still talking about it. It's just another lie that the DEA perpetrates to torment us. The District Attorney in Washington has to approve our transfers, and he ain't going to do that. He was supposed to be here six months ago to check out the prisons, and they're still talking about that too. Don't believe a word they say, they're all liars," he said decisively.

I had it all figured out, but couldn't help have my doubts. Twenty-five years was a lot of time, at the best-case scenario, and nobody had transferred on the treaty. There was no guarantee. As I pondered my fate, I met Mr. Kamul. Mr. Kamul prepared Chinese astrology charts. I'd never heard of such a thing. I thought it was probably another fortune teller scam, but I craved to know my fate. At no cost, he agreed to prepare a chart for me. He also explained that it was only a chart, and could only be seventy percent accurate at best.

To prepare the chart, he needed to know my first name, date of birth, and the exact time that I was born. It took three days to prepare, and was written in Chinese symbols. The symbols were lined up beneath the years of my life. He first related that my parents were divorced when I was eight years old—a fact that I wasn't sure of until I checked later. Skipping almost a decade, he knew when I ran away from home and moved to Kauai. "Not exactly sure, either sixteen or seventeen, velly close, not sure," he said in broken English. I moved to Kauai in October 1973, a month before my seventeenth birthday.

Four years later, he insisted that I cheated someone for a lot of money. This I firmly disputed. I considered cheaters as people who take advantage of others. That goes against my nature. I later learned that theft offenses are called cheating cases. It didn't dawn on me that banging cars was cheating, and the large score at the Pali Lookout was in 1977.

Skipping another decade, he insisted that I had a brother who died in 1986. *Strike-two*, I thought, I have three sisters and no brothers. I then realized that my grandmother died in 1986, when she was 96 years old. Considering that it was only a chart, I gave him the benefit.

Between 1986, when I was released from OCCC, through 1989, he accurately detailed everything that I did. "Why you do this business?" he asked, "You have everything, you no have to do this business. Now you have nothing and have to depend your family," he said, and then looked at the symbols in 1989. "You were here five months ago. Don't tell me yes or no, hundred percent sure you come to Thailand five months ago," he said.

I was in Thailand on February 14, Valentine's Day. I was arrested on July 10, five months later. I started to think he was connected to the DEA. However, he was serving a twenty-year sentence and had been in Bangkwang Prison for the past six years. Considering these facts, I eagerly awaited my future to be revealed.

The symbols were identical from 1989 through 1993, with only two symbols per year. When he examined them, he noticed a similarity from 1981 to 1986, when I was imprisoned in Hawaii, which he had initially skipped past. "Hey, same-same," he said, pointing back and forth between my past and future.

"What do these mean?" I asked.

"Not sure, either you make a lot of friends or a lot of money," he said, puzzled.

"Yeah, well, I was in prison before," I said with a chuckle. "But when do I get out this time?"

"No worly," he said, "Your thirty-seventh birthday you will go. Many good things for you. Hundred percent sure! 1994 is velly good year for you. Everything good come back, married, everything. No worly," he assured me. He made me promise that I wouldn't tell anybody. I kept my promise. Mostly because I'd sound flaky if I told anybody that this was my assurance of leaving within five years, as I had calculated.

My lawyer visited as promised. I planned on pleading guilty, so I only needed him as an interpreter. We negotiated a fee of $1000. After he left, Phil Lowenthal, an attorney from Hawaii, visited me with another Thai lawyer. The American Embassy called my mother in the middle of the night and told her that I was facing the firing squad. Hopeful to get me a fair trial, my family hired Lowenthal.

He first told me that EuroClassics was seized, and Wayne was arrested as a co-conspirator. Uncle Nick was working for the DEA, which I didn't realize until then, and a warrant had been issued before my arrest. The DEA had planned to grab me when I arrived home, but at the last minute they decided to let the Thais have me. Lowenthal had spoken to the District Attorney in Honolulu. He said that I wouldn't be prosecuted if I got a lengthy sentence and served a significant amount of time in Thailand.

"First we enter a not guilty plea," he said.

"Hold it. Wrong," I said, as I stopped him with my hand held up. "We're going in and pleading guilty."

"Do you mean you want to stay here in a Thai prison?" he asked.

"Of course not, but what choice do I have?" I asked. "It's either five years here in the tropics, or ten years in a cold, federal penitentiary. I mean, even if I did win, which I doubt I would, do you think the Feds would just take it in stride and let me go? Pleading not guilty means that I get dragged back and forth to court in chains, I don't eat all day, and the case drags on for years. The end result is that I get more time and he gets more money," I said, as I pointed to the attorney that he brought with him.

"Is that true?" he asked the Thai lawyer.

He silently nodded his head.

"But you're facing execution, what gives you the idea that you're going to be out of here in five years?" he asked, confused.

"If the laboratory weight is less than a hundred grams, then I can't get more than life. If I plead guilty, I'll get my sentence cut in half to twenty-five years, cut and dry. If I have anything less than life, then I can transfer home on the transfer treaty after I've served four years," I explained, as if it was all so simple.

"That sure is a lot of ifs," he chuckled. "Besides that, nobody's ever transferred on the treaty yet," he said. "It's too bad they don't have a plea bargain system here," he said as an afterthought.

"Yeah they do," I said.

"Really?" he asked.

"Yeah, it's called plead guilty or else," I quipped.

I put my confidence in Lowenthal and went with the attorney that he brought in. He wasn't any better or cheaper, just another shopping-cart attorney. Before they left, I gave him a list of food, toiletries and bed sheets that I needed.

After Lowenthal returned to Hawaii, I was paid a visit by the DEA. "Good morning, I'm Joe Bloesky from the Drug Enforcement Agency. I wasn't able to interview you at the airport, but our Hawaii office asked me to come down here to talk to you," he said, as he held his wallet open to show his badge. "I understand that you wanted to give us a statement."

"I never said that I wanted to give you a statement," I said flatly.

He turned to a Thai cop who was at the airport. They quickly conversed in Thai. "He said they gave you six pieces of paper at the airport."

"Yeah, they said they wanted a statement, I never said that I wanted to give them one. There's a difference you know," I said. "Besides that, what do you want from me? You got me already. I'm in jail. Should I just roll over, play dead, and sign my life away just like that?" I said, and snapped my fingers.

"No, well, uh, we could help you out at sentencing," he replied.

"Yeah right, give me twenty years instead of twenty-five. Doesn't sound like a very good deal to me, buddy," I said sarcastically. "Besides that, my lawyer doesn't want me talking to anybody unless he's present."

"Oh, you have an attorney?" he said with a smile. "What's his name?"

"Phil Lowenthal from Hawaii," I said.

"Oh really, I know Phil," he said.

"Oh really," I said, mocking his smile, "Good, go talk to Phil then," I said, and stood up to leave. Captain Krunch walked past as I turned towards the screened door. For theatrics, I turned around and gave the Feds the middle finger. "Aloha Oe and f... you assholes," I said, and walked out the door.

A few weeks later, I was indicted in Honolulu Federal District Court. The Thai case was linked with the Kastner case. The government confirmed that Uncle Nick worked for the DEA, under the cover of a confidential informant, and received the heroin filled shaving cream can from me on July 9, 1989. Without explanation, they stated that I was arrested on July 10, 1989 with the drugs given to him. You do the math. I may not be an Angel, but it's improper and illegal to be entrapped by my own government in a sovereign nation, and then delivered to the foreign government for prosecution and punishment. On the other hand, it's flattering to have the authorities go to extremes just to nail me.

Over a year later, I got Wayne's address and wrote to him in a federal prison camp in Oregon. According to Wayne, a SWAT team jumped out of the bushes with guns when he returned home on the day of my arrest. He was yanked out of a BMW by the hair and thrown against his fence. His six-year-old daughter and eight-year old son cried in horror as he was handcuffed. His house was ransacked. My fleet of cars was seized. Afterwards, he was held without bail. They charged him for the Thai case and the Kastner case, even though he didn't know Kastner or Brent. In fact, he didn't even know me at the time.

On the day of his trial, the Marshals told him that I'd been executed in Thailand. It became a rumor. The prosecutor approached him with a plea deal. "If you fight this case, I'll make sure you get ten years and you'll never see your kids again," the prosecutor said. His Public Defender silently cringed in the corner. Wayne cracked under pressure and pled guilty to the 115 grams that I was arrested with. He was sentenced to a mandatory minimum of five years. Unfortunately, there's no perfect system, and courts will always be a bummer. Thailand's courts are no exception.

Sentences for most crimes are lenient compared to drug offenses in Thailand. Bail isn't permitted in drug cases, and a defendant is guilty until proven innocent. The few who win have to wait until the prosecutor appeals it to two higher courts, known as second and third court. Drug cases drag on for years, unless you bribe the prosecutor to drop the case after the first acquittal. After a defendant is sentenced and all of his remedies are exhausted, the only hope for an early release was via an amnesty or King's pardon.

Amnesties were given every few years, honoring special occasions for the Royal family. The amount of time commuted by amnesty is based on classification. The classification process has five classes, from poor to excellent. Excellent class can cut a sentence by up to 50% every amnesty. Prisoners are given medium class when sentenced. If a prisoner remains trouble-free, his class is increased every six months. If he gets in trouble, it's decreased.

Rumors circulated every year of an amnesty being given. The administration was the source of these rumors, and sold class increases for a thousand dollars. In 1987, an amnesty included drug cases, but I was doubtful there would be another. George

H. Bush went on national television with a pound of cocaine and declared a "War on Drugs."

King's Pardons could be submitted after a few years. Allegedly, with the right connection, if the price was right, a bribe could secure a King's Pardon. Waterbed gave me a tip on Medical Pardons. For humanitarian reasons, the King granted Medical Pardons for foreigners with severe medical problems. He suggested that I go to the hospital every week on hospital day, even if there was nothing wrong. The hospital filled out an OPD card that kept a record of all visits and prescriptions. He also told me that the doctor prescribed Valium. It was a good back-up plan in case the transfer treaty fell through, and I could get high at the same time. I used my fractured spine as an excuse.

Every Tuesday, a doctor visited the infirmary from Lardyao hospital at Klong Prem. The infirmary was in a small building across the road from Building one. He issued me ten Valiums a week. A few weeks later, he discontinued the Valium and prescribed seventy Halcion. He explained that Halcion was the replacement for Valium. The only catch was that I had to fill the prescription at my own expense. I thought he was pulling my leg to give me the brush-off. No doctor in his right mind had ever prescribed me seventy pills similar to Valium, especially in prison. I had to give him the benefit of the doubt though, so I sent the prescription out with the American Embassy representative.

She promptly filled the prescription. Within a week I received the Halcion. I was sure that something was wrong when the Commodore gave me the entire bottle, along with the script back. Nobody would allow a prisoner to possess seventy mood altering pills, legal or not, I thought. To be sure, I washed five tablets down with my tea. I forgot my name, where I was, and everything else.

Prescription medication became my relief from boredom. I became a Halcion addict and used every excuse to get them. The doctor prescribed me as much as I wanted. He thought that I was crying wolf when I really got sick. Flat on my back in excruciating pain, my kidneys ached mercilessly. I freaked when I urinated blood. I had visions of being sliced up by a Thai doctor. The doctor said that it was from taking too many aspirin. All hope was gone. I literally thought that I would die in prison.

After a week of agony, Waterbed recalled a time when he had similar symptoms in Mexico. His doctor analyzed it as kidney stones, caused from drinking dirty water. I went back to the hospital and acquired a handful of green tablets that dissolved kidney stones. Within a few days I peed out a rock, curing the symptoms. I became my own doctor after that, and self-diagnosed myself from a Physicians manual.

Meanwhile, I was moved to Building two, where most of the foreigners lived. It was identical to Building three. We were let out at 6:30 a.m. every morning. At 4:30 p.m., we returned to our room. This gave us time to prepare meals with food purchased from the coffee shop. The embassy provided us with eight baht a day for food, the equivalent of forty cents. It was a provision for pre-trial prisoners. The coffee shop was a small room on the bottom floor of Building two, enclosed with a metal screen. Eggs, bread, and a variety of knick-knacks were sold at the counter, and could be purchased daily. A round of French toast was about a buck, so we pooled our funds and shared breakfast.

Bumbut housed drug smugglers from every ethnic group. The Chinese prisoners built an elaborate blue-tiled room with tables, chairs, shower and toilet. Thai servants waited on them hand and foot. Commodores brought them anything they wanted. Several Chinese were from the Hong Kong Triad. A Thai police chief was busted with forty kilos of heroin, and the nephew of Khun Sa was serving a one-year sentence at Bumbut.

Khun Sa is the General of the Karen army in Myanmar, formerly Burma. He established a territory in Myanmar known as the Shan State. Kuhn Sa was virtually untouchable and controlled the opium and heroin trade exclusively. The U.S. was pressuring him to seize opium production. As a consolation, he offered to eliminate the opium fields in Myanmar if funds for substitute crops were provided. The U.S. "Refused to deal with extortionists." Instead, a Federal Grand Jury in New York indicted him for importing several tons of heroin into the United States.

In 1993, the United Nations provided funds for substitute crops. By 2005, Khun Sa eliminated the opium fields in the Golden Triangle. China White is now unheard of in the region. The substitute crop now planted is 'ya-mah,' the key ingredient used to make methamphetamine.

Methamphetamine is the main ingredient in ICE, also known as crystal meth, batu, glass, clear and shabu. The penalty for ICE is ten times harsher than heroin, according to the Federal Sentencing Guidelines. For the first time in history, methamphetamine has taken over heroin as the drug of choice in Thailand. It's also fueling the ICE epidemic in Hawaii, which leads the nation per capita.

Khun Sa's nephew was an older Thai-Chinese with a sucked

up prune face. He probably smoked opium his entire life. Every morning he hobbled down to the infirmary to get his opium. The nurses provided him with an unlimited supply. Through an interpreter, we chatted every morning as he smoked his opium. He even gave us a small ball of it from time to time, which I dissolved in my hot tea.

Heroin was available, but using heroin or fighting bought a ticket to the Soi with chains. The Soi was a four by four-foot metal cage, the type used to airfreight German Shepherds. It was used for disciplinary segregation.

My last girlfriend in Chiang Mai wrote to me via my business address on Maui. My ex-girlfriend on Maui forwarded it with a sarcastic comment. I wrote to her in Chiang Mai and explained my situation. She must've had delusions of getting married and moving to America. Within a few months, she moved to Bangkok and visited me every week. It was nice of her to visit, and gave me something to look forward to. We weren't allowed to touch. Instead, we yelled back and forth through two sets of metal-screened bars, six feet apart.

After three months, I received the laboratory analysis. I was charged with exporting 99.5 grams, a half gram under the threshold. I now faced life instead of death. I hadn't heard from the attorney that we hired, so I wrote to him. I told him that I needed to talk about my case. He showed up a few days later. We didn't talk about the court case. There was nothing to explain. We talked about the case of Pepsi that I wanted him to buy for me. He also told me about the different types of bananas sold at the food stand. He was an expert on bananas.

We went to court and pled guilty. I was sentenced two months later. My girlfriend remembered that I drank Gin and tonics at the Hard Rock Café. She offered to bring a few to court when I got sentenced, as if it was an everyday thing. I couldn't think of a better escape from a day in Hell. Before court, I swallowed five Halcions. Everyone wears elephant chains for three months after they're sentenced. For a pack of cigarettes, the sledgehammer-man hastily pounded on a clean set of shiny chains. I cringed and feared the day he slipped.

At the courthouse, I hobbled out of the dungeon in bright orange shorts with a matching burlap shirt. The courtroom was across the street. Holding my chains mid-calf, I was led outside. In route, I passed my girlfriend near an outdoor food stall. She held a Gin and tonic in a clear plastic bag. It resembled a soft drink that was sold at the food stand.

She followed me to the courtroom and passed me the clear bag. I sucked it down in seconds. "More," I pleaded with a smile, and passed the empty bag back to her.

While she fetched another round, I waited in the courtroom. Another case was taking longer then expected, so I was moved to another courtroom. This gave me time to consume another round. The Commodore laid in a chair uncaringly as I sucked down the second round. The lethal combination of Gin and Halcions slammed me when I stood up in the docket. The Judge looked at me and babbled in Thai.

"Wha'd he thay?" I asked my lawyer.

"He said you've been sentenced to life plus two years," he replied.

"What!" I exclaimed, instantly sobering up.

"But reduced to twenty-five years plus one for entering a guilty plea," he added.

I received the extra year for the ninety-eight valiums that I was arrested with. The Judge didn't believe that they were legally obtained, "because I had so many." I found the logic to be ironic. I had been prescribed hundreds of pills in prison, yet 98 Valiums were excessive.

My girlfriend was shocked. She quickly calculated our ages. I'd be fifty-nine when I got out. She'd be forty-six. She couldn't wait. I bade her farewell, returned to the dungeon, and passed out on the dirty concrete floor.

Three Nigerians rode back with me on my final ride in the paddy wagon. They were arrested with forty kilos of heroin. The ringleader swore innocence in English. The other two spoke an African dialect. Only three Nigerians had been in Bumbut until then.

In October 1989, a month earlier, six Nigerians attempted to smuggle sixty-eight kilos of heroin out of the country in television sets. It was the largest heroin seizure at Don Muang Airport. One of the Nigerians was a woman. She was the only one caught. The five men beat-up the Thai cops and then ran away. This set-off a round up. Everyone black became a target.

Dubbed "The Nigerian Connection" by *Newsweek* magazine in a 1990 feature story, it exposed a major heroin route into the U.S from Thailand. From Bangkok, the drugs were smuggled into Lagos, Nigeria. In Nigeria, Customs were lax and bribable. From Nigeria, the heroin was then smuggled into New York.

Nigeria wasn't a profiled drug country, so couriers from Nigeria breezed through U.S. Customs.

CHAPTER EIGHT

NIGHTMARE IN BANGKOK

I hobbled down the cement road through Bumbut's maze of buildings. The chains gouged me as I walked. To alleviate the monotony, I consumed a pile of smack and a few Halcions. My sunglasses hung sideways as I clumsily carried my belongings. They could've been taking me to the gallows and I wouldn't have known, much less cared.

Divided by a large iron gate, I entered Klong Prem Prison, the infamous Bangkok Hilton at Lardyao. Klong Prem was built for prisoners of war during the Japanese occupation in World War Two. Robbers, murderers, pirates and rapists were all integrated within the population of over ten thousand drug addicts and traffickers. I was taken to Section two, my new home. Another large iron gate bordered the section. Hollywood met me at the entrance.

Hollywood was a heavy-set ganja smuggler with a walrus mustache. He resembled a pro football player. Lowenthal, who represented one of Hollywood's co-defendants in America, informed him of my arrest. His chuckle after looking at me said it all. Once inside the section, Hollywood took me to the American hut in the "Garden."

The Garden simulated a Viet Cong village. It was originally an acre-sized pond, called a klong. Rainy season submerged the entire section every year, filling the klongs with mud and raw sewage. After the floods subsided, a landfill was created from the dredged sludge, forming an island, which became the Garden.

To the right of the Garden, a large klong remained intact. The rest of the Garden was surrounded by narrow klongs. Small scum-eating fish gasped for air near the surface. The fish were a Thai delicacy, and the klong was drained bi-annually to harvest their catch.

A bamboo gate marked the entrance to the Garden, known as Junkie Junction. Dry brown palm-thatched huts lined both sides of a potholed cement path, which lead through the middle unto the back strip. A sewage trench flowed parallel to a high cement wall topped with rusted barbed wire. Bumbut was on the other side of the wall.

Tucked away in a corner near the slop and garbage pit, to the right of the back strip, was the bath and toilets. Two squat toilets drained the crap directly into the sewage trench behind it. The bath was a four by six-foot cement trough, centered between the garbage/slop pit, the squat toilets, and the raw sewage trench. Enough to make you puke, the combination of atrocious smells produced an indescribable stench when the sun heated it up. At first I couldn't understand why the entire place always stunk, and the flies swarmed around the dirt and plants. I discovered that the Thais used human waste as fertilizer, and the open bins of fertilizer contained my last crap.

Through an overhanging purple bougainvillea bush that covered the roof, I entered the American hut. The hut rested on a cracked cement slab, atop a garbage-filled klong. A bamboo retainer wall kept the hut from falling into the klong. A large cherry tree to the left of the entrance shaded a small garden of tropical plants that bordered the neighboring huts. Woven mats and plastic rice bags served as dividers between the other huts. What really caught my attention was "Ollie North," a tall, slim, fit, all American looking square dressed in a Boy Scout uniform.

"What are your intentions while you're here?" he demanded, after he saw how loaded I was.

"Don't worry man. I know I'm a little f...ed up, but I didn't want to bring any dope over from Bumbut, so I consumed it all," I said, when I realized that we had the nicest pad in the Garden. "But while I'm here, I plan to take it easy and won't draw any heat on you guys."

Ollie was one of the last major ganja smugglers busted in 1987. He didn't fit the drug smuggler profile though. Hollywood nicknamed him Ollie North because he was so straight. He didn't smoke pot, yet pushed tons of it. When he got arrested, he broke down in tears. He thought it was impossible for him to get busted. I couldn't see how it was possible. Thailand was the hottest drug country in the world.

The Blue-shirts ran around the Garden and blew their whistles at 4:30 p.m. The day was over. "Evelybody go yo rooms," they shouted in-between whistles.

"It's the Chinese fire drill," Hollywood said, "Time to go back to the kennels."

I hobbled into the T-shaped cellblock in my elephant chains. Two hundred foreigners lived on the second tier. Most of them lived in cells that were fixed-up at their own expense. As a new arrival, I slept in the adjoining wing. My first few weeks were spent in a grayish-black, mosquito infested cell. The cell was eight feet long and barely six feet wide. The last two feet was the bathroom. A short wall separated it from the sleeping area. Crammed in with three Thais and an Arab, the five of us slept on the cement floor widthwise. The only accommodation was a 60-watt light bulb that shined in my eyes all night. Those who greased the Building Chief's palm occupied their own cells. The rest of the cells housed three prisoners or more. To prevent murders, two prisoners per cell were prohibited. How or why I don't know.

Sobering up the following morning, I had coffee with Dan and Hollywood in Dan's small hut next to ours. Dan was a slim, older Brit who looked like a banker. I thought he was an embezzler. It turned out that he was a ganja smuggler with an organization known as the Marco Polo gang. Dan was fighting extradition to the U.S. He was indicted under the Federal Racketeering Statutes (RICO) for marijuana importation charges that spanned decades. He was also wanted in Australia, Canada and Britain.

"So what's the deal with Ollie?" I asked Hollywood. "Is he always that weird?"

"Yeah man, that was a trip yesterday," he said, chuckling. "You should've heard him Dan, he sounded like a PIG, and Android over here was f...ed up and slobbering. It was classic," he said, still chuckling.

"Don't laugh, it wasn't funny," I said. "I've been in some radical prisons before, but that was heavy."

"Don't worry man, you're my guest," Hollywood said. "Just be careful what you say, I think he's working for the DEA. He's doing fifteen years now, and they're king-pinning him for twenty-five tons that got busted off Hawaii last year."

"You're kidding. I read the story in the *Honolulu Advertiser*. I think the ship was the Christina. Over twenty guys got popped on that one, and they mentioned someone that was imprisoned in Thailand. Was that him?" I asked.

"Yeah, he was the financier, happened while he was here. Why do you think he's a Blue-shirt? He bribed the Vice-Commander to get the job. He can leave the section anytime and ride around the prison unnoticed. That's his cover to visit the DEA in private," Hollywood said in a whisper.

"Wow, that's spooky man. Isn't that like espionage or treason, or something?" I asked.

"Fraternizing with the enemy is the way I see it. There's a war going on, and we're the POW's," Hollywood said with conviction. "You better talk to Rock, he's the veteran here."

"Who's Rock?" I asked.

"Rock's from Little Rock. He's in the Soi with twenty other guys. They had a little gang-fight in Loui's kitchen," he said, as he pointed to a lean-to attached to the front of the American hut, about twenty feet away.

"Oh yeah, I heard about that. What happened anyway?" I asked.

"It was pretty heavy. The Chinese and Westerners haven't been getting along. Me and Dan were sitting over here and heard all this noise and clanging. We had front seat view. Knives were slashing, faces were cut up, bamboo clubs were pounding heads like watermelons, it was nuts. A few of the French got stitches on their faces. Blood was everywhere. Now they're in the Soi licking their wounds. Only God knows what Loui served for dinner. I'm just glad he's not my cook," he said.

"Where did they get all the knives from?" I asked.

"You kidding, everybody has knives. How do you think we eat?" he said, chuckling. "They took 'em away for now, but we'll get them back after the dust settles. I still got a few, and Ollie's got a butcher knife if you need it. Don't worry we've got everything," he assured me casually. "In the meantime, you should talk to Rock. He's upstairs in the Soi," he said.

"Where's the Soi?" I asked. "I didn't see any dog cages."

"The Soi isn't like the Soi at Bumbut," he chuckled. "Over here, they keep us in our cells with chains," he explained. "Give the Blue-shirt a pack of cigarettes and he'll let you in the building."

Loui's Chinese kitchen was a fire hazard waiting to happen. Loui fed all who were too lazy or incompetent to cook, including me. He served char siu ribs, roast duck, barbecued chicken, fried rice, and an assortment of other Chinese dishes out of his lean-to restaurant. Loui was a skinny Chinaman with a rattled brain. He was semi brain-dead from too many heroin overdoses. His only comprehension of English seemed to be, "Yo mama." If he wanted something, "Yo mama." If my food was ready, "Yo mama." Everything was, "Yo mama." I could imagine him landing at LAX and calling a black porter to carry his luggage.

Loui was from Hong Kong. He was one of many Chinese

spread out in the Garden. They came from every country in Asia. At the time, there was a division between East and West. The racial remarks were different from the ethnic humor in Hawaii. The Chinese are a significant part of the local culture in Hawaii, and bigotry is all in fun. Locals from Hawaii are colorblind. Now considered a westerner from America, I found myself stuck in an identity crisis.

I moved out of the dirty cell within a few weeks, and moved in with Tojo. It became my permanent home for the duration of my stay. Tojo was a quiet, well-mannered Japanese guy my age. He lived in a cell by himself. To live alone, he had to pay rent. Tired of being squeezed, Tojo moved in two cellmates, Goofy and me.

Goofy was a Dutch-Indonesian from Holland. He could've passed for a Hawaiian beach boy with his tanned skin, Polynesian looks, and black shoulder length hair slicked back. I nicknamed him Goofy, because he was good-humored and always smiling. In turn, he called me dopey because I was always stoned. Goofy owned a casino in Amsterdam. He had served six years in a Dutch prison prior to this, and was waiting to be sentenced for possession of fourteen kilos of heroin. To avoid a death sentence, he pled guilty.

It was a perfect arrangement. Tojo taught me basic words and phrases in Japanese that we practiced in our cell. "Ocha, desu ka?" (Do you want tea?) Tojo asked.

"Hai, atsui ocha o kuda sai, arigato gazaimasu," I replied, (Yes, hot tea please, thank-you very much).

The American hut was centered amongst every nationality in the world. People came and went all day. Ollie was our American translator. He spoke French, Spanish and Thai fluently. The only common ground that Ollie and I had was through Chess. Chess is a game of strategy that I associate with life. I became a skilled player while in Oahu Prison. Ollie was a beginner. To gain his respect, I taught him different moves and strategies.

"Touch move," I said, "You know the rules. If you touch it, you move it."

"Why? We're not playing in a tournament," Ollie protested.

"No. But we're playing chess, and that's a basic rule. If you want to learn to play right, then you have to move the piece that you touch. If you take your hand off it, then it stays there," I instructed.

"You're just saying that because that's the only way you can win," he sniveled.

"Yeah right," I scoffed, "I can beat you with one eye closed while I'm stoned."

"Bullshit asshole. Let's play another one then," he demanded.

"Nah, that's it for me. You're too uptight. Besides that, it's almost time for my Sunday brunch," I said. "Hey Loui, yo mama," I shouted towards the woven mat divider.

"Yeah, yo mama," Loui yelled back, "Five minutes, five minutes. Yeah yo mama, I make velly nice for you. Five minutes," he said.

"Yeah O.K., yo mama," I said.

I paid Loui $100 a month to prepare a decent Hong Kong style Chinese plate every afternoon. My only other meal was noodle soup for breakfast. It was my daily task. Holding my chains mid-calf, I hobbled up the path between the huts to the coffee shop.

The coffee shop was another lean-to on bamboo poles, outside of the Garden, and across the klong from the French huts. Meat, vegetables and fruits could be ordered on Mondays, Wednesdays and Fridays. Paid in advance, it was delivered the following week. Bread, ice, toiletries and kanams (sweet Thai snacks) could be purchased over the counter. The costs were deducted from a 'Pink Card,' and signed for the following morning. Pink cards were the only legal currency. All money deposited on our books through the embassy, visits, postal money orders, etc. were entered in Thai baht on the pink card.

Cash was contraband, but everybody had it. It could also be purchased from the coffee shop. 650 baht was subtracted from the pink card for 500 hundred baht cash. 500 baht, $20.00, was the largest Thai note. Cash could also be picked up from the bank or visitor by a Commodore, and then brought in for a ten percent surcharge.

Cigarettes and Tam Jai were other forms of currency. Tam Jai was a small yellow packet that looked like a lottery ticket. It was a Thai energy booster worth one baht. It contained a high sodium powder that tasted like Japanese meat tenderizer. The Thais swallowed it like a sugar packet.

Cigarettes cost 150 baht per carton—ten packs—at an outside food stand. Visitors could purchase food or cigarettes at the stand, and then have them delivered inside. A carton of cigarettes were sold on the prison black-market for 120 baht, the equivalent of $5.00. Cigarettes were re-sold in the coffee shop for 20 baht per pack; a forty percent mark-up. If you didn't have money, cabbage soup was the only alternative.

Daily at noon, a welfare line of third-worlder's lined up at junkie junction for the cabbage soup. On Saturdays we got one raw egg. It was the only food provided to foreigners by the embassies. The Thais rationed out a bowl of dirty rice and a watery mixture of cabbage with pig entrails. Inedible by western standards, it was a diarrhea enhancer. In exchange for my clothes being washed, I bartered out my rations to a Burmese refugee.

Washing clothes was a hustle the Burmese marketed. It was their key to survival. Clotheslines were attached to every tree in the section. Amongst other oddities, a variety of colorful French underwear flapped in the wind. The bright red and blue panties were a hot-commodity. They were snatched off the clothesline by the Thais, and sold on the prison black market to the Katois. Katois were Thai transvestites.

Rock was released without charges on Christmas Eve, along with the other foreigners involved in the gang fight. It was settled with a bribe to the Building Chief, known as the Building Thief. It was his New Years bonus. All problems within the section could be settled with a pay-off to the Building Thief. To celebrate, Rock busted out a slab of hash, and Hollywood smuggled in a few bottles of whiskey.

Rock was a hippy-type biker with a ponytail. He was serving a twenty-year sentence for heroin smuggling. His father was a 4-star General stationed in Thailand during the Vietnam War. Rock grew up in Thailand during the war, and spoke Thai like a native. He also had his share of interesting stories.

"How'd you get twenty-years instead of twenty-five?" I asked him, "I thought that twenty-five years was the lowest you could get for heroin."

"Because I had 18.52 grams, less than twenty grams is a maximum of fifty years. With a guilty plea it was reduced to twenty years," he said. "Actually, I had 185.2 grams, but we got the decimal point moved over a digit at the laboratory," he said in a whisper. "This makes it easier to get a King's Pardon. I'm just waiting on it now," he explained, and showed me a copy of his pending pardon.

Another poor little rich kid, I thought, familiar with the entitled feeling. Additionally, his mother was the secretary for Governor Clinton of Arkansas. Rock's mother had spoken to the Governor about him. She had it arranged for him to work with drug prevention programs upon his release. Knowing Rock, he probably screwed off the opportunity, not realizing that Governor Clinton would become president.

"When I first came in, there was only forty-seven people in the whole Garden," Rock said whenever a new arrival came in.

"Don't worry Rock, I'll be saying, 'There was only a hundred and thirty-five people in the Garden when I first came in'," I said, mimicking him, as an increase seemed inevitable.

Herman Munster was a tall, awkward, French-Canadian, who walked stiffly and resembled Frankenstein. He came in with a Pakistani, and built the first hut in the deserted strip across the klong from us. It was the start of a building boom.

The Spanish nut hut was behind the cherry tree. Rock had a nickname for all of them. Dracula was a scrawny hunchback with receding hair greased back, and a large wart on the side of his nose. Rambo was a child molester about fifty years old, with a crew cut and a variety of cartoon tattoos on his legs, arms and back. Explicitly noticeable was a large red tongue tattooed to the back of his thigh, captioned, "KISS MY ASS." Jimmy Durante was an old buzzard about seventy-six years old, with a long beak and wrinkled face. He couldn't speak English, so he communicated by making gestures with his eyes, and shrugging his shoulders. Mariano was a big Spanish junkie with long straight black hair, mustache and acne infested face. He looked like he would cut your throat in a second, but was actually a pretty nice guy.

The Spanish nuts lit their fireplace and fanned the smoke towards us every morning. Loui ignited his barbecue barrel and blew it our way also. We got fumigated. The entire hut was filled with smoke. When the smoke cleared, it was time for the Thai national anthem.

The anthem sounded like the Mickey Mouse song played with a kazoo. It's a serious ritual obeyed throughout the country. At 8:00 a.m., traffic on the streets of Bangkok comes to a halt, and nobody walks or talks while this neurotic tune is played.

Blue-shirts ran around the Garden with whistles. All of the foreigners were rousted from the Garden. If we didn't stand for the anthem, we were put in the Soi. The foreigners lined up single file along the well-mowed field outside of the Garden. The Thais lined up in rows on the cement sidewalk near the chow hall. An army of Commodores surveyed the rank and file of misfits. Those who didn't sing along were firmly tapped on their shoulders with slim black Billy-sticks. Then the day begins. The Thais go to work in the factory. The foreigners return to the Garden.

The factory was a building outside of the Garden near the coffee shop. The Thais made spoons, nails, paper boxes and other odd items sold in mass production to private companies. They were worked tirelessly, for twenty cents a month. Those who didn't make their monthly quota were given a few lashes with the cane.

The cane was a thick dry bamboo stick, about four-feet long. It was used on the Thais for various reasons. Up to ten lashes was common. Fortunately, they didn't cane the foreigners. It would probably spark a major outcry—by me. Hit on the back of their thighs below the butt, the Thais got walloped. I watched many men buckle.

"Cop coon cup (thanks a lot for the cracks)," they said after a caning, and bowed with their hands clasped together.

Of the hundreds of Thais who were caned, only one stood defiantly with his arms folded across his chest. The Commodore wound up like he was hitting a home run. A loud CRACK slapped his hamstrings. He refused to acknowledge the pain. He was given ten of the hardest lashes I'd seen. He wouldn't give them the satisfaction. He was a bull. He gave a short nod to the Commodore afterwards. In return, he got a smile of respect from the Commodore, and a loud round of applause from the crowd of foreigners. He also wore a rainbow of deep purple and green bruises across the back of his legs for several weeks, a common sight after a caning.

For an hour a day, the foreigners were required to make plastic flowers in the factory. The plastic flowers were long stemmed pink roses that had little tags attached to them. The tags described them as "Handmade in Thailand." They were sold on Fifth Avenue in New York. I saw it as slave labor, so I wrote messages on the tags. "HELP! I'm a prisoner in Thailand. I'm being forced to make these flowers. Please call my mom," and I'd include my mom's phone number. The tags soon disappeared. This routine got old quickly, so I bribed the Commodore to take me off of his list.

My self-appointed job and hobby was taking care of the garden around our hut. It was a trade I learned as a pakalolo farmer on Maui, and a routine that I enjoyed. I planted, watered and manicured my botanical garden of small palms, rubber plants, vines, ferns and hanging orchids everyday. The cherry tree shaded it well, and the purple bougainvillea bush that covered our roof added color. My garden became enviously lush, and brought life to our gloomy world. Our hut looked like an arboretum, but still smelled like a cesspool.

Tojo also appreciated plants and flowers. He had a rare orchid that took three years to bloom. When it did, he showed me a magnificent, large, purple, sweet fragrant orchid. It also had a sweet perfume aroma which is unusual. They're usually an odorless flower. It reminded me of my grandmother, the one who died in 1986. I bought her a large purple orchid for Christmas in 1978, which was the last time that I saw her. I knew that it was rare, because it was expensive. It also had a fragrance. She adored it, and it made her Christmas.

Shortly after moving into Tojo's cell, I was abruptly awoken by the loud shrill of a train's whistle. I immediately sat upright. A distinct déjà vu feeling hit me. The midnight train from Chiang

Mai arrived at the Lardyao train station, outside to my right. I instantly flashed back to the nightmare that I dreamt. *DAMN*, I thought to myself, as I pounded my fist against the wall. I realized why I had recognized the train when I met it in Chiang Mai. Was it a warning or was it destiny?

It became a re-occurring nightmare every morning at 4:30 a.m. I could hear it a mile away, as it traveled from my right towards my left. It then turned towards the prison, and slowly chugged towards me. The scenario was identical. Every morning its whistle blew as a reminder. After awhile, the joke got old.

It raised several questions that I tried to figure out. Everyone has experienced a déjà vu, the distinct feeling of re-experiencing an experience. On the average, we spend a third of our lives sleeping. Most dreams seem to be forgotten when we wake up, but the memory never forgets anything. It's just not recalled. When we have a precognitive dream, we recall it when it reoccurs—déjà vu. The experience is the recall. My nightmare was so intense that I remembered it clearly when I dreamt it. When it reoccurred, I knew why I had the déjà vu feeling. This served as my assurance of being released by my thirty-seventh birthday, and convinced me that God has a plan for my life. Knowing that everything happens for a reason, I started to write. It was the only purpose in God's plan that I could find. Ironically, I flunked English and hate to write, but definitely had the time.

There wasn't a day that went by where I didn't question what reality was. Klong Prem was another dimension. It was a cross between a circus and a zoo. Chickens, ducks, turkeys, guinea pigs, rabbits and cats roamed freely within the Garden.

"Is this all real?" I asked Hollywood, as we both stared at the abnormal world around us.

He shook his head and chuckled. "No, it's just a bad dream," he said.

"Thanks, I just wanted to make sure," I said. "Just wake me up when it's over."

CHAPTER NINE

THE GARDEN

I heard an eerie, howling echo through the building at sunrise. I thought the Commodores were torturing someone. The howling continued until I heard, "Shut the f... up you bastard! Some of us are trying to sleep." It was the beginning of Ramadan. The Muslim's prayed towards Mecca four times a day, and ate before sunrise or after sunset.

Most of the Muslims were Middle-easterners from Pakistan. They held a Muslim mosque in the building at one o'clock every Friday afternoon. Muslims from other sections were allowed into the building for the service. Security was tight. The visiting Muslims secreted heroin in their anal with a string attached to it. In turn, the Paki's from Section two greased their okoles beforehand. Once inside the mosque, they prayed behind their brother and made the hand-off. The stash was then smuggled into the section up a different okole.

Abdul was the Paki connection. He was our last resort to score. Abdul was a short Paki about five-feet tall, with a thick mustache, wild wavy hair, and whip scars engraved down his back. If I were anywhere else, I'd check to see if my wallet was lifted. The Paki's built a pole-house over the klong in front of our hut. A

Paki wrapped in a tablecloth, with a rag around his head, sang in an off-pitched tone. Six Paki's sat in a circle fluttering their eyelids. We had front seat view.

I wore a wool sweater one morning. Abdul was fascinated with it. "What kind of jacket is this?" he asked.

"It's not a jacket," I replied, "It's a sweater, a wool sweater."

"Wool?" he asked puzzled, "What is this wool?"

"Wool," I said again, "You know, material made from sheep."

"You mean, you make this from sheep?" he asked, amazed.

"Yeah, sure. Why? What else would you use sheep for?" I asked, and then thought about it for a second. "Never mind, don't tell me."

Thailand was predominantly a Buddhist country. Christmas and Easter went by as just another working day. Chinese New Years was according to the Buddhist calendar, which originated 553 years before Christ. Chinese businessmen donated rubber slippers, toothpaste and soap to all of the prisoners every year. This would bring them a prosperous business year.

Thai New Years followed Chinese New Years. Customarily, the Thai tradition was to be thrown into the klong for "good luck." Blue-shirts lingered by the gate of the Garden and waited for victims to come out. Foreigners were snatched by the arms and legs before they knew what was happening. In the old, one-two swing, they were tossed into the dirty klong sideways. My good luck was being able to escape this ritual every year.

The only practicing Christian was Sonny. He resembled Buckwheat of the Little Rascals. Sonny was one of three Nigerians in the Garden when I arrived. He had been there over ten years.

He swept the floor of our hut and washed our dishes. This was his hustle to survive. Everyday at noon, he spent an hour in Sonny's Chapel. His church was a phone booth-sized lean-to near the corner of the Garden. I should've been following the Lord, but drugs were an easier route.

We got visits from European missionaries regularly. They served as runners to the stores, and brought us the latest in pirated videos sold in Bangkok. Every weekend, we watched videos in the TV hut. It was the only time that we were allowed electricity in the Garden. The TV hut was a ten by ten shack in the corner of the Garden. The foreigners paid to have it built, and chipped in for the TV and VCR. A chair had to be bought. It was a permanent chair. When the owner left it was re-sold, and the money would be donated back to the kitty.

The Paki's were the first to watch movies every Saturday morning. Paki movies had no plot. Waterbed was the only westerner during Paki movie time. He liked to watch cartoons. Paki movies were close. The Chinese followed with Kung Fu movie time. The westerners were last. English videos played for the rest of the day. The only time that I didn't watch the flicks was during hot season.

Hot season began in March, and lasted through April. A Hawaiian summer was cool next to hot season in Thailand. The TV hut became an intolerable sauna. It was over a hundred degrees in the shade, literally. There wasn't a breath of wind. The humidity was unbearable. Flies thrived on the putrid stench of garbage cooking in the hot sun.

Rainy season followed hot season, and turned into Monsoon season. It started in May and lasted through July. Swollen thunderclouds blanketed the sky and hovered over the Garden. Noon turned into evening. A cool wind blew in. Bright flashes of lightning illuminated the huts. The sound of thunder exploded in a loud BOOM. Torrential rains poured down. Howling winds tore apart the dry palm-thatched huts. Everyone scrambled for high ground. Cats cringed under the lockers, yelping out terror-stricken cries. The klongs instantly filled up and overflowed throughout the section. The section was flooded a foot deep within the hour.

Our hut was built over a foot above the ground, keeping us from being submerged. The rest of the Garden went under. Snakes surfaced amid the raw sewage and fish. It gave me the chills when they squirmed beneath my footsteps. A squished turd between my toes was worse. A thunderstorm was the closest we got to a real shower. The Garden became a male nudist camp. In-between downpours, we sprinted to our cells for the night.

The deafening echo of thunder vibrated the cellblock throughout the night. A strong wind blew through the building. Power shortages knocked out the electricity. I loved it. It was the only time that we slept with the cell light off, and the cool breeze was comforting.

The morning after a thunderstorm, I administered first aid to the plants around our hut. Hollywood and Ollie boiled water over a small clay stove. It was our only source of drinking water. The fire was fueled with charcoal purchased from the coffee shop, and fanned with a cardboard box. Our meals were also cooked over a clay stove. Meat could be purchased from the coffee shop, but the beef, referred to as buffalo, was too tough to chew. Instead, we ate a lot of chicken.

After three months, my chains were pried open. The skin was scraped off both sides of my ankles. The infections took months to heal and left permanent scars. It was a relief to move around. I could walk and run again. It felt like I had been freed. I now learned badminton.

We had two courts set-up every morning. The wind was calm before 9:00 a.m. It was the best time to play. Hollywood and I were partners. We became badminton fanatics. The Chinese were the ones to beat. Teams waited their turn. We played sets or two out of three. Losers got out.

Others played Takraw. Takraw is a popular Thai sport that I called soccer-style volleyball. Similar to volleyball, but without using hands, they kick and head-butt a small bamboo ball over the net. The Europeans and Nigerians played it with the Thais. I didn't even try.

All sports were played outside of the Garden. Others had an exercise routine, which included Yoga, Kung Fu or walking around the perimeter of the section. The Thais weren't allowed in the Garden, so the Junkies walked around the buildings in search of a drug connection. This was no-mans land, known as Front Street. To score from the Thais was dangerous. "If he's a Thai, he's a spy," we said, because they turned us in at every chance.

"Hey Andy," Hollywood called out, "You up to any badminton this morning?"

"Yeah sure, let me finish watering the plants though," I said.

"Right on. How are your ganja plants doing? Are they still alive?" he asked.

"Nah, f...en Ollie keeps pulling them up, being the pig he is," I said.

"Really? What an asshole, we outta kill that bastard," Hollywood said.

"You're telling me," I said, as I dropped my water bucket. "O.K., wait. I'll put on my shoes and meet you out there. Go get it set-up."

Everyone was waking up and having coffee as I walked up the strip of wall-to-wall palm-thatched huts that led to Junkie Junction. "Jo-son ho, Buddha. Ohio, Yoshisan. Goota morgan, Adolph. Buena's Dias, senors," I said, as I walked past. "Sawadee cup, how's yo mama?" I said to the Blue-shirt at the guard post near the entrance.

"Sawadee cup," he said, smiling. He didn't understand English.

"What are you doing out here, Landshark? Are you going to play badminton this morning?" I asked Solomon. Solomon was an energetic and talented Jew, who spoke at least six languages fluently. He was the main drug dealer in the Garden. When he was high, he ran around the Garden non-stop. He could be heard shouting and whistling from across the klong or through a hut. The next minute he'd appear through a bush.

"Yeah, no, uh, kind of, wait I'm trying to pick-up. There's the shit now, he just dropped it over by the bush in that toothpaste box," he said, and looked around from his left to right.

"Be careful man, there's Blue-shirts everywhere on Front Street this morning," I said.

"Don't worry I've got it under control. Oh shit. Here comes a Thai with a dustpan and broom. Mama Mia! He just scooped up my stash and dumped it into his garbage bag," he cried, and then took off. He grabbed the garbage bag out of the Thai's hands, dumped it upside down, snatched the toothpaste box, and sprinted back to the Garden.

"You crazy f...en Jew," I said afterwards. "How you pull off those suicide runs and not get busted is beyond me."

"Hey man, you just gotta be fast. What else could I do? The f...en Garden's dry, everyone's sick, and the only shit around is about to be thrown away," he said.

"Huh, huh, huh, you're heavy man. Well bust it out. What are you waiting for? Let's see if it's real or not," I said, nudging his arm.

"Wow man, I don't got that much right now, let me sell it first so I can get more," he said.

"F... you! What are you, a Brooklyn Jew or something? Come on man, I thought you were a Jew from Israel. Get that cork out of your ass, let's get down," I said.

"F... you, O.K., what you want, sniff or chase the dragon?" he asked me.

"Chase the dragon of course. We ain't got nothing else to smoke. Here I've got some tin foil in my locker," I said, as I got everything prepared.

Flaming a lighter beneath the tin foil, with crumbs of heroin on top, we inhaled the rising smoke until it evaporated, giving an instant high. Smoking heroin was an occasional novelty. Intravenous usage was the unwritten no-no. The threat of AIDS was taken seriously after numerous inmates tested positive. The Blue-shirts also patrolled the Garden on the lookout for dope, so everyone was extremely cautious with it.

Bumbut filled up with Nigerians, which we learned by word of mouth and the sporadic copies of the Bangkok Post that filtered in. To alleviate the overflow, all large drug cases were transferred to Klong Prem. That's when the first tribe of Africans arrived in the Garden.

"Holy cow! They busted the L.A. Lakers," Hollywood exclaimed in jest.

"Lakers. It looks like they busted the Rams too," I added. "See the last two guys. I saw their picture in the *Bangkok Post*. They had forty kilos of smack."

"Man, they'll die in here. They gotta do away with those f...en chains though. Poor guys look like slaves in bondage," Hollywood said.

"Yeah that's sad," I said, relieved that I no longer wore mine.

A lot of the Nigerians were professional boxers, weightlifters, and drug kingpins. The kingpins had larger amounts of up to forty kilos. They were intelligent, cool, always smiling, and had enough money to survive. I called them the Brotha's. Others were fresh out of the bush mules without a dime to spare. They were paid a couple of hundred bucks and a new pair of shoes. Most had swallowed up to a kilo of heroin in balloons.

Waterbed and Captain Krunch were also transferred to Klong Prem. Waterbed bought a light purple painted cell and hung a Jimi Hendrix Poster on the wall. It was his "sixties hippy pad." In the corner was his guitar. He didn't know how to play it.

Krunch moved into Solomon's cell. Solomon was a Jew from Israel. Krunch was a Jew from Brooklyn.

"I can't believe it. This bastard is stingy," Solomon said after he lived with Krunch for a month. "All my life I thought it was a joke about Jews being stingy. He's sick. It's a disease. It's ugly. Never in my life have I met anyone as stingy," Solomon said, incredulously. "Are all Brooklyn Jews like this?" he asked me.

"I don't know, I'm from Hawaii, we don't have Brooklyn Jews," I said, and chuckled at the irony.

Solomon didn't know the meaning of impossible. Israel didn't have a transfer treaty, so he needed a King's Pardon. Feigning appendicitis, Solomon was taken to the hospital and given a urinalysis. He pricked his finger with a needle and squeezed blood into the urine sample. Doctor Jon, the head doctor, ordered him to be hospitalized. Once inside the hospital, Solomon bribed a doctor into switching his blood test with an AIDS patient. He immediately filed an AIDS Medical Pardon, and was pardoned a year later.

The American Embassy was supposed to visit us once a month. We didn't count on it. Sometimes we didn't hear from them for several months. Any visit was welcomed though. It was our only connection to the outside world.

I received an unexpected visit from John and Tracy, a young Californian couple staying at a guesthouse in Bangkok. Guest houses posted the names of foreigners in Thai prisons. The visit was a pleasant surprise, and opened me up to a real side of people. They were traveling around the world on bicycles, so we corresponded throughout their journey. I was given day-by-day details of their bike trip. They described their adventures into Northern Thailand, and on through Laos, Vietnam, Malaysia, Singapore and Indonesia. I felt as though I was traveling with them. John's family lived in Switzerland. They biked to Europe through Czechoslovakia, Poland, Austria, Hungary and Switzerland. They stopped in Switzerland for Christmas, and sent me Swiss chocolate and cassette tapes.

My younger sister Claudia also visited a couple of times. She worked for Aloha Airlines and could travel for free. She surprised me on my birthday when I was in Bumbut, and visited again during the inside-visit held in August 1990. We had special inside-visits twice a year. Visitors could come inside, and were allowed to bring food, clothes and toiletries. She carted in two large boxes of food and clothes. The Commodore started to search everything. It would've taken him forever.

"Here," she said, and handed him a bag of Oreo cookies.

"For meee," he asked.

"Yeah, for you brah," she said sweetly. He stopped the search and waved her in. The two-hour visit was the highlight of my nightmare. Claudia was the only member of my family who could make the trip to Thailand. She was the sister who came to me in my nightmare. We were also allowed food, clothes, books and magazines through the mail. To keep up with the world, my other sister, Jeanne, bought me a subscription to *Newsweek*.

Goofy's partner mailed him a hash menu from Amsterdam. It advertised various types of hash sold in a Dutch coffee shop. Thailand is famous for its Ganja, but hash isn't manufactured there. The Thais didn't know what it was. Goofy had a hundred grams of black primo hash mailed to me in a parcel. The hash was mixed with chopped fruits to look like a fruitcake. Cookies and other food items were included in the parcel.

Within a few weeks, I was escorted to the prison post office by a Blue-shirt. Twenty Thais stood around waiting for their parcels. Blue-shirts rummaged through the parcels on the lookout for white powder. Sitting in the hot sun with my back propped against the wall, I waited for my name to be called.

They opened my parcel, and snacked on the cookies and chips inside. Using a utility knife, a Blue-shirt sliced the gooey slab of fruit/hash in half. I cringed. There were pieces of hash mixed everywhere. It was too much to hide. My goodies were inspected within seconds and slid over to me. They promptly dug into another parcel. I couldn't contain my excitement. "Kop koon kup" (thanks a lot), I said.

Tojo and I separated the hash from the fruits in our cell that evening. Goofy didn't use drugs, which I found ironic. Amsterdam is the most liberal drug country in the world. Tojo persuaded him to smoke a joint with us. It was a one-night fling for him and a rare treat for us. We ate and smoked hash until we passed out.

The following morning, I surprised Hollywood and Dan with a few handfuls of hash saturated fruit. "What the...Wow! Right on dude," Hollywood exclaimed. "Where'd you get this?"

"Never mind, shut-up," I said. For the rest of the day, we ate everything in sight. The secret was out after I gave a joint to Frank, a Nigerian boxer who looked like Joe Frazier.

"Hey Andy, can you sell me a joint?" asked Mike, a huge super-cool Nigerian weightlifter, after he got the word an hour later.

"Sell you a joint? Why, do you got money?" I asked, although I knew he didn't.

"Not now, but I'll pay you later," he said.

"Yeah right," I said laughing, "Don't worry man, it's on me," I said, and gave him a chunk of hash. "Stretch it out though, and share it with the Brotha's."

"Thanks man, I will," he said, and skipped out the door.

Ganja and hash didn't create a problem. It was the least of all evils, but the Commodores didn't want to smuggle it in. They couldn't make as much money from ganja as they did heroin. Ollie didn't object when we smoked it. He'd leave the hut when we lit up though. My main concern was to pull easy time. His main concern was to buy his way out of there. I didn't think it'd ever happen.

"If you have a thousand dollars, I can get your classification increased to excellent class," Ollie said, in-between chess moves one day.

"A thousand dollars," I scoffed, "Why would I want to do that?"

"Because there's an amnesty coming up," he said. "If you have excellent class, you can get your sentence cut in half."

"Yeah right," I said sarcastically, "Spend a grand so my twenty-six years will be cut down to thirteen, IF there's an amnesty, and IF it's a full cut, what good will that do me?" I asked, as I moved my queen in for the kill.

"Because your sentence will be cut in half again after the next amnesty," he said.

"That'll bring me down to six and a half years, when I can leave on the treaty within five," I said. "Check," I said firmly, putting his King under fire.

"You're so stupid," he said, irritated. "There may not even be a transfer. It's not guaranteed."

"I'm so stupid? Amnesty, scamnesty, if I had an extra grand, I'd spend it on ten grams of heroin before I threw it away on classification," I retorted. "Checkmate," I said, as I captured his King.

In May 1990, America initiated the first treaty transfers. Three American men were released to the custody of the U.S. Bureau of Prisons from Bangkwang Prison. They had served eight years. Upon their return, they were released on parole under the Pre-1987 American Parole Guidelines. Those guidelines provided immediate parole to prisoners transferred from foreign prisons if their crimes had been committed prior to November 1987. The spirit of transfer treaties is to allow foreigners alternative incarceration in their home countries, opposed to the harsh conditions found in third world prisons. The Thais didn't foresee it as an avenue of release, and complained about their release.

A prisoner's release differed per country. Although the treaty was initiated by America, treaties with Thailand had also been ratified by France, Canada, Britain, Spain and Italy. The first group of French also transferred in 1990. Others countries soon followed. Goofy was sentenced to life and moved to Bangkwang Prison. Tojo was pardoned. Rock was also pardoned by the King. He became the last American to be pardoned while I was there.

When Tojo left, he gave me his rare orchid plant. To create more of them, I transplanted and separated it into four pots. Afterwards, I hung them on the corner of our hut. They seemed to thrive, but didn't bloom.

In 1991, an amnesty was declared in honor of King Rama V. He freed the slaves in the fifteenth century. The reduction was a third-cut for excellent class prisoners. All drug cases were excluded.

"Well it looks like they didn't include us in the amnesty Ollie. What's up with that?" I asked him.

"They decided not to give one this year, because it was only a third-cut," he said. "Next year is going to be a bigger amnesty for the Queen's 60th birthday, so they can give a full 50% cut."

"Yeah, right, with the transfers rolling, I doubt if there will be another amnesty for drug cases, especially with the drug war going on," I said.

"No they're not. You're so stupid. You haven't seen an amnesty before. I was here when they gave a half-cut in 1987," he said, blowing his top as usual.

"Yeah, that was before. This is B-5. You're out of touch with reality idiot," I argued.

"You're suffering delusions," he said. "They'll have an amnesty before any more transfers."

"Yeah, right, with my luck we'll probably be transferred back together," I said.

"That would be the day. Besides that, I'm not even going to apply for a transfer," he said.

CHAPTER TEN

BARREL OF JUNKEYS

"Yeah, I just seen my Embassy Bitch," Josie said, irritated. "She keeps jaggin' me off about transfers and pardons. I told her she's a worthless cumbucket," he said, as if it was a cool thing to tell her.

"You called her a what?" I asked. Hollywood and Dan broke out in laughter.

"Why? What's so funny? Isn't that what you guys told me to tell her?" he asked. "By the way, what's a cumbucket?"

Tsang Tak Tsing, known as Josie, lived with Dan and Hollywood. Josie was a high-ranking member of a Triad in Hong Kong. He spoke at least six languages fluently, and was traveling on a Filipino passport under the alias Jose, which he pronounced as Josie.

Hollywood, Dan and Josie ran the coffee shop. Nelson was their accountant. Nelson was a short, skinny Filipino my age, and the smallest guy in the Garden. He was a Merchant Marine. While docked in Thailand, a drunken crewmember beat him and then tried to stab him. Nelson turned the knife on him as they struggled. The knife pierced the drunk's heart and killed him. Unfortunately, Thai law doesn't recognize self-defense. Nelson pled guilty to murder and was sentenced to nine years. Nelson had a good sense of humor, so I moved him into my cell when Tojo and Goofy left.

"Speak English, I can't understand you," I teased, because he pronounced his P's and V's, like B's.

"Yeah, I spick English," he said, indignantly. "What you tink, hea? I spick berry good Amerdican standord English."

Secano also moved into my cell. Secano was a tall, slim, well-mannered student dissident from Myanmar, formerly Burma. He fought for democracy and lost. The military murdered and jailed countless students. To evade arrest, he fled Myanmar and crossed over into Thailand. The Thais arrested him for illegal entry. Secano was humble, but naïve, and a target for our humor.

"Hey Nelson, you forgot to feed the cows," I said. The bullfrogs belched out loud "Moos" whenever it rained, which sounded like a pack of cows.

"No, I not suppose to feed da cows, this time your turn," Nelson said spontaneously.

Secano climbed on top of the squat toilet divider wall and looked through the cell window. "Huh? Where da cows?" he asked, curious.

"Over there by the trees. Can you see them?" I said.

"No. Where?" he asked, looking intently into the dark.

"What you tink stupid, get cows?" Nelson said, as he rolled in laughter. "Ha-ha-ha, no more cows, only frogs, ha-ha-ha-ha."

Our evenings were spent talking about our lives and different places in the world. I learned a lot about the Philippines from Nelson. The climate is similar to Hawaii and has over 7000 islands. It also has some of the best surf in the world. A thousand Hawaii's is the way I saw it. I always wanted to spend some time there, but had been there only once on a stop-over. When I arrived, I thought the Customs counter was an information desk.

"Do you have any alcohol sir?" asked a classy Filipina girl, who resembled a stewardess in her blue uniform.

"Alcohol? No," I said.

"You're allowed two bottles duty-free," she said. "Can you buy me two bottles of Johnny Walker Black Label," she asked, and handed me a ten-dollar bill, "And just put it over here," she said, pointing to a corner behind the counter.

"Yeah sure, no problem," I said, and then bought her the two bottles. When I returned with a duty-free bag, I placed it behind the counter and smiled as we made eye contact.

"Welcome to the Philippines sir," she said, and promptly stamped a thirty-day visa into my passport.

I liked her style. It was my way of doing business. Bribery is an acceptable way of life in Asia. "Straight corruption" is how Nelson described it. If you paid a bribe, you could expect delivery. Everything has a price in the Philippines. I dreamt of buying an island, surfing my own break, and having topless babes on the beach.

"If you could go anywhere and do anything, what would you do?" I asked Nelson.

"My dream is to pick apples in America," he said.

"Pick apples?" I asked, chuckling, "Are you crazy or what?"

"Yeah," he said, "Why not? That is my dream in life, if only I could go to America and pick apples. You stupid Americans don't know how lucky you are. I can only dream pick apples, you can do anytime," he lectured me.

"I guess I never thought of it that way," I said. "But there's a lot of things you can do in America."

"No, I want only to pick apples. Philippines no have apples. America has plenty apples," he said, serious.

Nelson was exceptionally smart. He knew everybody's name, pink card number, amount of money they had, and everything that they bought. He was also quick witted. He walked through the Garden every morning and had us sign for our purchases. "Money! Who you? Ha-ha-ha-ha," he said to anyone who questioned his memory.

Through the coffee shop, contraband could be smuggled into the section on the food cart. Hollywood and Dan offered to give me sixty grams of China White heroin on credit, at a hundred dollars per gram. It was a junkies dream, especially in prison. However, when the dope arrived, they gave it to Captain Krunch instead. He had the cash up front. I didn't. I knew that he would screw it up. He was clumsy and careless in everything that he did. Hollywood didn't listen to my advice though.

Krunch divided twenty grams into balms and papers. I buried the remaining forty grams in my garden. Balms were small tiger balm tins filled with a third of a gram, sold for 1500 baht, $60.00. Papers were small magazine bindles one-fifth the size, sold for 500 baht, $20.00.

As I expected, he got busted before the first twenty grams were sold. The Blue-shirts were waiting for him by the squat toilets. They rushed him when he made the corner. He had ten papers in his hand. He kicked one of the Blue-shirts and shoved the dope in his mouth. They pounced on him and shoved raw crap into his mouth to make him spit it out. Shit was smeared all over his face as they took him to the Soi. It cost him a few months in the Soi and $4000 to have the charges dropped. A cheap bribe compared to the cost of an inside case. In the meantime, Hollywood and Dan had to get rid of the remaining forty grams that I buried.

"Hey Andy, can you get rid of the rest of the stash?" Hollywood asked me. Dan sat on the side.

"Ohhh. Now you want to be friends huh?" I said, facetiously. "I could've gotten rid of it before, but you didn't want to listen to me. Now Krunch is in the Soi and the heat's on. What's going to happen if I get busted? Are you going to pay my way out, or am I going to suck?" I asked.

"Look," Dan said, "We've got you covered. The Building Thief gets his envelope, and he calls off the Blue-shirts. We'll give you the smack at the same price, and we'll pay the squeeze. If you keep it cool, we'll give you fifty grams a month, uncut."

"Every month, uncut?" I asked.

"Every month, guaranteed," Dan said.

"You've got a deal," I said, and we shook on it. I sold the remaining forty grams, kept a low profile, and soon received fifty grams a month. For the following year, I supplied the entire Garden and a generous habit.

Dan was a financial genius and brilliant with numbers. He made a regular profit at the coffee shop. Dope increased those profits. Selling cash multiplied those profits. Dope had to be paid for in cash, but I gave credit to a select few. Those with shaky credit had to see Dan for cash, or buy cigarettes at its inflated cost. A typical scenario was when Mariano bought a paper from me.

"Andy, I'm sick. Can you give me a paper on credit?" Mariano asked.

"Sorry, I need the cash. Do you got any money on your books?" I asked.

"Yeah, I got boom-bom, plenty. I just don't have cash, and they want to break my balls selling me cigarettes. C'mon man, help me out," he pleaded.

"I'll tell you what, make out an IOU for six-fifty baht. If Dan will guarantee it, I'll give you a paper. In fact, here he comes now, let's go ask him," I said.

"Dan, can I get 500 baht for a six-fifty cut from my pink card?" Mariano asked him.

"Yeah sure, where's the IOU?" Dan asked, as the three of us stood in a circle.

Mariano handed Dan the IOU. Dan gave Mariano a 500 baht note. Mariano gave me the 500 baht and I gave him a paper of smack. I then handed the note back to Dan. "Can you deduct this from my tab Dan?" I chuckled, knowing that he just made a quick 150 baht.

"Yeah, no problem," Dan chuckled, as he put the 500 baht note back into his pocket.

Prior to lockdown at 4:30 every afternoon, I made drug transactions on the tier fronting my cell. This was the busiest time of day. Waiting for a fix is an addict's worst nightmare, and the fourteen-hour lock-down was a long time to go without drugs. There was still a division between the Chinese and Westerners, so I didn't realize how many Chinese were strung out on heroin. Lu Chi Fai, known as Six-fingers, had double thumbs protruding from his right hand. He was the smallest one in the bunch.

"I'm solly, I no have money. Can you help me? I'm sick," he asked me. His nose was runny. Misery was written on his face. I didn't know him, but I knew the feeling well and respected his honesty. Most junkies lie through their teeth and promise the world when jonesing. I quickly made up a large paper of smack and gave it to him before lock-down. We became friends and he never forgot the favor. I later learned that his brother ranked #2 in the Hong Kong Triad. Six-fingers always had a lot of money, and was one of the few that could be trusted. I gave him a thousand dollar line of credit.

The fifty grams per month were sold in three weeks. This left us in misery until the next load arrived. The Thais had heroin intermittently, which buffered the wait. Other foreigners found ways to smuggle in dope, but were scared to sell it. Instead of taking a chance, they sold it to me.

Jumbo and Kong had connections throughout the prison. Jumbo was a large Buddha-sized Chinaman. He was the financier, but couldn't speak English. Kong was a skinny Chinese from Hong Kong. He spoke English, Thai and Chinese fluently. They were scared to hold onto ten bottles of heroin, so they fronted it to me. I was stoked. The Garden was dry and I was sick. I paid them promptly and in full, which led to other deals.

The Chinese were the only ones that I could trust on a handshake. Jumbo became my Chinese brother. I supplied him when I had it. He supplied me when I didn't. He sold to the Chinese. I sold to the Westerners. It was a mutual agreement. Through drug deals, we closed the ethnic gap. The circus went on unabated for so long that it became business as usual. My connections eventually included the Chief of Security on down. Everybody had a price.

The Garden became divided between the junkies and the non-users. The non-users stayed in shape by lifting homemade weights, jogging, walking, etc. However, they were vulnerable to the rampant diseases such as worms, T.B., hepatitis, and etc.

The junkies outnumbered the non-users. The only time a junkie was sick was when he ran out of stash. Heroin's a vaccine that keeps an addict immune from most illnesses and pain. Created in 1890 by the Bayer aspirin company, Heroin is the pharmaceutical name of their "miracle cure-all drug." It was the main ingredient in cough syrups and aspirin. Heroin was outlawed in 1915, under the Anti-Narcotics Act, along with cocaine.

Hollywood and Dan didn't use heroin. They were strictly ganja smokers. Hollywood detested junkies. He called us a bunch of losers. Dan could care less, as long as he made a buck. Consequently, Hollywood became curious and turned into a closet junkie. I made chokers for him to smoke on the sly. He was worried that Ollie and Dan would discover his weakness. It started as an occasional fling. This fling led to once in the morning, and again in the afternoon. Before I knew it, he became a monkey on the loose. It was my gravest mistake, and soon had to support two King Kong habits.

I continued going to the hospital every week. Every Wednesday morning was hospital day for Section two. Anyone who wanted to see the doctor lined up at the front gate. Everybody wore blue colored shirts, the color required outside of the section. If you didn't have a blue shirt, a blue burlap bag was provided. I wore a blue Polo shirt.

Thirty foreigners marched down the wide cement road single file, whistling the tune from "The Bridge on the River Kwai,"—the movie of the Burmese death railway in Northern Thailand. Klong Prem was a little city. It was divided into ten sections. We strolled past Section one, three, four and five. A Blue-shirt led the way. Spacious lawns filled the expanse between buildings. Short well-trimmed hedges obscured the sewage-laden trenches bordering the road. Blue-shirts and Commodores rode by on bicycles. Large trucks drove through. Ollie rode around on a girl's bike with a little bell, saluting every Commodore that he passed. Unarmed Commodores walked around holding hands. I thought they were gay. I learned it was normal. In route to Lardyao hospital, we passed the mailroom, the Vice-Commander's hut, the visiting room and a troop of female impersonators—Katois.

Thailand was the tuck and roll cosmetic surgery capitol of the world. There was no shortage of Katois. They smiled, waved and shook their butts while passing. Section four housed the Katois. They were segregated from the main population. The prison's food was also prepared in Section four, making me wonder what other foreign ingredients were added to the cabbage soup.

We entered through another large iron gate. Inside was a two-story clinic, Lardyao hospital. Three rows of narrow wooden benches under the stairs served as the waiting room. The doctors were interns, fresh out of Medical school—quacks. Banking on a prison quack was Russian roulette if you needed an operation. Even anesthetics weren't free.

Prisoners arrived at Lardyao hospital from Bangkwang prison, under heavy guard, with handcuffs and ten-kilo chains. Prior to his execution he's given a physical. He's sentenced to die by gunshot, not heart attack.

A trip to the dentist was a valid excuse to see the doctor for sedatives afterwards. Cavities could be filled for a reasonable price, but you got what you paid for. Pulling teeth was their specialty.

A dozen junkies sat on the benches with a shopping list of drugs written out. I had received hundreds of Halcion by this time. I now learned about other pharmaceutical drugs, including a sedative called Rohypnol. Rohypnol is highly addictive and the tolerance quickly escalates. A normal dose will induce a comatose sleep for twelve hours. It was later known as the 'Date Rape Drug.' Women were drugged with it on dates. It's now banned in America and Thailand.

I had a collection of excuses for the variety of drugs that were prescribed. I needed verification of my injury for the Pardon that I planned to file, so I contacted the doctor in Hawaii who performed the surgery on my spine. He sent a letter verifying and detailing the injury. Feigning severe pain, with the letter in my hand, I slowly entered the doctor's office hunched over and holding my back. "Doctor, I need morphine," I said, grimacing as if in severe pain.

"I'm sorry, I don't have morphine. What else can I give you?" he asked. "Oh, uh, just fifty Temgesic for pain, fifty Valiums to relax, and fifty Rohypnols so I can sleep please," I said, and handed him a slip of paper with my order written down. Twenty other foreigners stood in line behind me. Orders in hand, stories rehearsed.

My tolerance escalated to four Rohypnols a day, in addition to my heroin habit. Every evening, I crushed a Rohypnol and mixed it with an equal-sized dose of China White. It was technically an overdose. After sniffing up the mound of white powder, I smoked a choker to enhance the mixture. In a deep nod, cross-legged in the corner of my cell, I slept sitting up every night. At 5:00 a.m., I came out of my coma and went right back to the tin foil. After chasing the dragon, I made up balms and papers for the morning circus in the Garden.

Since we served most of our time in our cells, I had Yak, my key-boy, make a bookshelf for me. He securely mounted it on the wall. In the middle of the shelf was a one-inch divider that spun around like a false bookcase. The divider was kept in place by two screws. To fill the safe, I took out the screws so it would spin around. The drawer was in the back, and was big enough to hide my money and stash. Nobody ever discovered it.

Yak had a big tiger tattooed across his chest. He was one of the few Thais that I trusted. He was sentenced to twenty-years for two contract murders. "Litnoi" (little), he said, knowing that he'd be out in less than ten years via amnesties. He was one of eight key-boys in the building. The key-boys had a designated set of keys for each wing of the T-shaped cellblock, upstairs and downstairs. Yak didn't speak English, other then the dirty words and slang that I taught him. "Hey Andy, you stupid f...ed up asshole," was his favorite one-liner.

Room searches were conducted every couple of months. We were never caught off-guard. The Chinese Blue-shirts tipped us off the night before. A squad of Blue-shirts, led by a few Commodores came in at 5:00 a.m. We stood outside of our cells while the Blue-shirts searched the rooms. The search was brief. I had eight bottles of pills on the shelf. They didn't even look at them. Instead, they flipped through a book, lifted a pillow, and then picked up my picture frame. When they left, Yak re-locked us back in. "Solly, go back sleep," he said, and handed me a paper filled with smack.

The huts in the Garden were searched afterwards. We fed the squad cookies, candy and other goodies. Those who didn't pay bribes were the only ones targeted. When they finished, a whistle was blown, and F-troop scurried out of the Garden. Without a moment to spare, lockers flew open.

Spanish junkies lined up in the Spanish hut. Mariano made a few lines and chased the dragon. To my right, a dozen Chinese huddled in their shooting gallery. Lookouts stood watch at every corner. Amid a chorus of "Do leh lo mo," they consumed a pile of China White. Across the klong, Herman Munster lay in his chair cock-eyed, mouth wide open, stoned out of his tree. "Yo Ma-ma," called out from behind the bamboo curtain. I sat in my lounge chair and chuckled. Ollie sat at the table fuming.

The Hong Kong hut was ten steps away, in an open-air hut to our right. I called them the Hong Kong Triad. It was in the corner of the back strip, enclosed by a flimsy bamboo rail. A multitude of Chings, Chongs, Wings and Wongs lived in the Hong Kong hut. We had a birds-eye view of the action. It was always full-tilt. They didn't seem to know where they were, and somehow found a way to get whatever they wanted. A dozen Chinese played Mah Jong and shouted excitedly in Cantonese. Jumbo sat on a rice can and made papers from his locker. A pile of smack sat openly on his shelf.

When the stash ran out, the Garden became dead silent. The energy level died. The junkie monkeys became powerless. Nobody slept a wink. I had constant diarrhea and threw-up all night. At 6:30 a.m., I dragged myself down to the Garden and squatted over the porcelain hole. The dysentery-type pain from the squirts was unbearable. The squirts were rinsed with dirty water. "Hold with your right, douche with your left," became tradition.

Glued to my chair, my only comfort was watching everybody else die. We chuckled at each other's misery. The only driving force was hope. Jumbo perched on top of a short log protruding from the klong with joss sticks (Asian incense) clasped between his palms. He prayed for the stash to arrive. Like hawks, eyes were on each other. Flickering left to right, watching and waiting, we waited day in and day out.

Josie hooked up with the Thais, and brought me five balms concealed in Tam Jai packets. I opened my locker with a smile on my face. Relief could be sensed in every direction. Josie hurried out the door to get more. Hollywood collected cash at the door. He sold papers quicker then I could make them. The Garden suddenly came to life. Laughing and singing in the cold shower filled the air. Pale white faces turned colorful. Appetites were suddenly restored.

Dan was still fighting extradition to America. Thailand and the U.S. didn't have an extradition treaty. His release was ordered three times, but they wouldn't let him go. The Thais snatched him from Klong Prem one morning. Hollywood got a letter from him later. He was in custody in Dade County, Florida.

With Dan gone, my China White supply dried up. He was the moneyman that kept the coffee shop afloat. Hollywood was strung-out big time. He couldn't stop. Instead of taking care of business, he scored dope to feed his habit. His funds dried up, the Building Thief stopped getting his envelopes, and the coffee shop went bankrupt. Eating cabbage soup became a reality.

"What are you doing, Hollywood?" I asked.

"Eating cabbage soup, what's it look like I'm doing?" he growled back.

"Yeah, how is it today?" I asked facetiously.

"Taste like shit! What do you f...en think?" he snapped back.

"Any meat, fish heads maybe?"

"F... off asshole, I'm hungry. What else is there to eat?"

"I don't know. I've got Loui cooking me up some fried rice with sweet and sour pork," I said. "You want some?"

"Right f...en on," he said, and threw his cabbage soup into the klong. "Why didn't you tell me sooner?"

"I don't know, I thought you were enjoying your fish heads," I said.

"Yeah right, when's that crap ever enjoyable?" he said, disgusted.

Hollywood's habit drained him of every penny. He was in debt up to his ears. Hollywood initially paid his lawyer $250,000 to get him off the hook. Instead, he got the max and never saw his lawyer again. After a few years, his outside sources stopped sending money. The Chinese bought the coffee shop, and Hollywood was kicked to the curb. Jumbo took over the show in the Garden.

I sat in my lounge chair with a cup of coffee every morning and waited for the circus to begin. Willpower was a fantasy. It was a miracle if I lasted until 8:00 a.m. To escape the monotony, I got a massage on the Thai side of the section. "How much you massage me?" I asked a Thai masseur, mimicking a massage with my fingers.

"Noong shamon, noong buri," he said. I didn't understand a word he said. The language barrier was always a nuisance. After finding an interpreter, I got a complete massage for a pack of Krong Thip cigarettes (50 cents).

CHAPTER ELEVEN

THE YEAR OF THE MONKEY

A colorful show of fire rockets exploded in mid-air at midnight. It was the first full moon of 1992, Chinese New Years—The Year of the Monkey. The entire city of Bangkok erupted in fireworks to chase away the evil spirits. New Years endorsed a drinking spree for the Commodores. They stumbled around the section slobbering and slurring. The Chinese prisoners celebrated in style. A magnificent display of roasted duck, pig, chicken and fruits were set up in the Hong Kong hut. Money was no object. Everyone was invited.

"A very dangerous year," according to Mr. Kamul, 1992 was the only year that he forewarned me of. "You born Year of Monkey," he explained, "You same like monkey, clever, fun, anything you like do. This year same like monkey, cannot predict. Maybe velly lucky, cannot tell, maybe bad luck. Be velly careful. This year velly dangerous," he said.

Chinese astrology is based on twelve-year cycles. They believe our personalities imitate the animals designated to the year we were born: Rooster, Dog, Pig, Rat, Ox, Tiger, Rabbit, Dragon, Snake, Horse, Ram and Monkey. Marriages, birthdays, business deals, and all-important decisions are planned according to

Chinese astrology.

Thai New Years followed a few months later. Pro-democracy students had a clash with the military in the streets of Bangkok. The army opened fire into the crowd with machine guns. Over eight hundred and fifty students died in Thailand's version of the Tiananmen Square massacre. Hundreds died in puddles of blood. Bodies were thrown into parked cars, set afire and cremated. The rest were tossed into dump trucks and carted off to an unknown remote jungle, never to be seen again. Thousands of students were beaten with clubs and rounded up. They were taken to Klong Prem Prison and dispersed amongst each section, including Section two. TV's, radios and newspapers were immediately blacked out.

They were kept incommunicado in cells most of the day, but were brought out to eat. Hundreds of students filed into the caged Thai chow hall. They had cuts, lumps and ripped bloodstained clothes. Fed the red rice/slop eaten by the Thai prisoners, I watched them flinch with sour expressions on their faces. It reminded me of my first gourmet meal. We conversed through the chain-link screen of the chow hall, and got a first-hand account of the drama that went on beyond the walls. They recited a startling tale of being stampeded by students and club wielding soldiers.

The government covered-up the death toll. They claimed that only fifty were killed, and eight hundred were missing. Facts proved differently. Doctors found human remains in burnt cars, and the missing children have never been found.

A few days later, the King pardoned all of the students. They were immediately released from Klong Prem, and the media blackout was lifted. The King publicly admonished the Prime Minister on live TV. He was then banished from the Kingdom of Thailand. This was extremely rare. The Monarchy is a figurehead that doesn't interfere with the government. Nobody ever knew who really ran the country anyway though.

The Queen of Thailand was born in the Year of the Monkey. An amnesty was declared honoring her 60th birthday, her fifth cycle in the Year of the Monkey. It was a major celebration. A fifty percent reduction was given off all sentences, except drug cases. 50,000 prisoners were released under this amnesty. This allowed Nelson, Yak and Captain to be released. They were all in for murder.

Captain was the Captain of a Burmese pirate ship. He was convicted of murder and piracy. Captain was respectable, polite and always smiling. I'm sure that the dialogue would've been different if I were sailing. Pirates in Asia are ruthless. They throw men overboard, and then rape the women and children. It's a common occurrence in the Gulf of Thailand. As a non-drug case, his sentence was commuted several times via amnesties. He served only eight years.

People came and went, but the drug smugglers remained. By this time, the Thai and U.S. governments had approved Captain Krunch and Waterbed's transfer applications. Hollywood's was deferred a year. Ollie didn't apply to transfer. He expected to get his sentence cut in half from the amnesty. He had also invested in a Pardon. He allegedly had the "connection." I assumed that he was getting taken for a ride, but didn't need to prove that I was right anymore. Time was taking its toll on all of us.

The African population increased dramatically. Tribes of Africans packed the palm-thatched huts around us. Congo music played all day. They argued consistently, usually over food. Most didn't speak English. All I could grasp was, "Ooga-booga."

The klong in front of our hut was clean with live fish until the Nigerian Connection moved in. They poured garbage, slop and dirty water into the klong as if it was a running stream. The fish vanished, and the klong turned into a black mosquito infested swamp. It smelled like a raw sewage treatment plant. To resolve the problem, the Thais filled the klong with fresh garbage. It became the new landfill. Droves of large black flies swarmed over the stench-laden garbage pit. Our waterfront pad became a repulsive, fly-infested, garbage pit. Black sticky spots of fly shit speckled the entire hut. It was unbearable.

The flood of Nigerians didn't slow down. The round up continued. In an attempt to elude arrest, one African jumped off of the airport's roof. Another dove out of a hotel window. It was sad. They walked around the Garden with broken legs, arms, and brain damage.

I asked one of the brighter ones why he came to Thailand. "Didn't you know what was happening here?" I asked.

"Uhh, yeah man. I knowed about da people getting busted and stuff, but I thought they must've been stupid," he said, as if he was one of the smarter ones. I can't say that I'm any smarter though. I was in the same boat.

The AIDS epidemic flourished rampantly within the prison. Thailand became one of the largest infected countries in the world. AIDS prisoners were quarantined in an AIDS Garden, until an AIDS Ward was completed at the hospital. The AIDS Ward was a secret vaccine program that used prisoners as human guinea pigs.

Martin was a black American from Chicago. He didn't know that he had AIDS until he had a leg injury that wouldn't heal. He tested positive when he went to the hospital. The American Embassy didn't intervene.

"I brought out you're EMDA loans today," announced the Embassy representative, after we wheeled Martin into the visit room in a wheelchair.

"Well," Martin asked in-between gasps for air, "Do you think I'll live long enough to pay it back?" Within six weeks, the disease devoured him.

A lot of prisoners died of AIDS and other diseases. Some died from lost hope. A Nepalese died of a stroke, and a Chinese died in his cell from an asthma attack. Two older Malays who were arrested together, died together. They had served over fifteen years and expected to be released for the Queen's birthday. They were brokenhearted when the amnesty excluded drug cases. A few weeks after the amnesty, one of the Malays died of a stroke in the hospital.

A week later, his partner had chest pains and requested to see the doctor. He had a heart attack as he waited at the front gate. Hollywood saw him collapse and fall on his face. Blood was all over his face. Hollywood ran over and called a Commodore for help.

"Ha. Fighting, fighting," the Commodore said, after he saw the blood.

"No man," Hollywood said, "He had a heart attack, he needs help."

"Ha, fighting, fighting, no good," he repeated.

"No fighting. Heart attack. Go hospital," Hollywood said angrily.

"Ah, ma be lai (no problem), take him Garden," the Commodore ordered.

Hollywood dragged the guy back to the Garden, several hundred yards away, in the hot mid-day sun. "Hey Andy," he shouted, "Give me a hand, this guy just had a heart attack!"

Before I could help, the Malay had another heart attack. Hollywood held him up so he wouldn't fall on his face again. He had a scared look on his face. His eyes rolled, he gasped, and then died right in Hollywood's arms.

"God dammit! Those mother f...ers just killed another one," Hollywood swore, "We could've saved him, but all that mother f...er could think of was fighting."

Hollywood was pissed. In an American prison, a prisoner can be treated properly and immediately. In Thailand, all you could do was pray that you didn't get seriously ill. Even if you're able to get to the hospital, chances were slim that you'd get diagnosed properly. A prime example was Paul.

Paul was a California surfer serving a life sentence at Bangkwang prison. He had served four years by this time, and could've transferred if he hadn't fought his case. Instead, his nightmare had just begun. Paul had a stroke at Bangkwang Prison. They didn't have a hospital there, so he was transferred to Lardyao hospital. He was in a wheelchair. The right side of his body was paralyzed, and his vision was fading dramatically. The doctors ruled out any possibility of a stroke. They said it was psychological, not physical, and sent him to the Lardyao nut ward. The only remedy was the electric shock machine.

I met Paul in the hospital after I had a confrontation with a Singaporean gang over a twenty-dollar food bill. They attacked me from behind, and stabbed me in the hand. My index finger was sliced at the base. I thought I was going to lose my finger. I made a bandage with an old rag and asked the Building Thief to transfer me to the hospital. Instead, I was accused of fighting and locked in the Soi with chains. The Singapore gang was moved out of the section.

The following morning I was taken to the hospital. Using what looked like a household needle, my mangled finger was stitched up Rambo-style by a Thai nurse. Taking her time, she pulled five stitches through my finger as if it was a leather bag.

"What, no anesthetics?" I asked the tall, flat-chest nurse with bucked teeth and round-rimmed glasses.

"No, you suppose to bring yourself," she said, impassive.

Six weeks later, I bought the investigating Commodore a bottle of whiskey. They dismissed all charges. In the meantime, this ordeal aggravated my spinal injury. Three weeks later, I was admitted to Lardyao hospital.

I was moved into Ward Two, the operative ward. After being tested for AIDS, I was laid up on an old wooden planked bed with a thin mattress. The sheets had bloodstains. It smelled like death. My roomies were prime candidates for a mercy killing. The guy to my right smelled like a dead dog. His legs were black, crusty, swollen and paralyzed. He lay there decaying. Nobody dared to give him a sponge bath. The stench of decaying flesh and rotten crap was a smell beyond description.

The guy on my left had bullet holes in his spine, butt and left leg. He had a little shoot-out with the cops. I think they blew his balls off too. His left leg was paralyzed, and he had a tube attached to his cock. His leg was amputated the next day.

The guy directly across from me was down to bones. Hooked up to an IV bottle to one arm and a bottle of blood to the other, his lower half was a skin-covered skeleton. He had sticks for legs. His hipbone was totally meatless. It stuck four-inches out of his side like a stick shift. His entire butt and thighs were bandaged in a diaper. The Thai prisoners acted as medics, and warded off the swarming flies with bug spray. I don't know how much longer he lived, but I didn't give him a week.

The healthier patients walked around with slit throats and bloody gauzes around their necks. I spent my nights fighting off mosquitoes that buzzed in through the huge holes in the screens. Fat rats scurried around chasing cockroaches. The perpetual stench of urine, crap, puke and decaying flesh was indescribably gross. Complaining to the doctor about the conditions was useless.

"You must learn to adapt to your environment," he told me.

You've got to be kidding, I thought. What's scary is that I wasn't dying when I went in, but the possibility was real. Stiffs were carted out practically daily. At first I couldn't believe it. After awhile, it was no longer traumatic to see dead people lying around. The meat wagon pulled up every morning. The medics took a few pictures of a corpse out in the open, and then casually tossed the body into the back of a Toyota truck. If someone died on a weekend or holiday, the body is left in a hallway off to the side. The meat wagon picked it up on the first weekday.

After reviewing my X-rays, Dr. Jon recommended I file a Medical Pardon. It appeared to be his way of soliciting a bribe. I was flat broke though, so we left it at that. After a week in the hospital, I returned to Section two and filed a Medical Pardon. It was my back-up plan in case I didn't get transferred on the treaty.

After suffering over fifty joneses, the withdrawals outweighed the pleasure. I seriously wanted to stop using heroin. The physical pain and suffering lasted three to five days, not including the insomnia and craving that dragged on for a month. By the fifth day, after suffering another insomnia-riddled night of hell, my strength was returning and I felt better. I was determined to make it my last jones. I put on my sunglasses and went to the Thai side for a suntan. While soaking up the sunshine, Jumbo strolled by.

"You want to go Hong Kong?" he asked. "Come inside, five minutes." Easier said than done, I folded up my lawn chair and went right back without hesitating.

In a sudden move, Jumbo and Kong were moved to Section five. A squad of Commodores and Blue-shirts came in and grabbed them. They were strung-out to the max, but didn't have time to smuggle any dope out with them. Forced into a jones, I could imagine the suicidal feelings that they must've experienced. By 5:00 a.m., Kong could no longer endure the torture. He hung himself.

We assumed that he rationalized his fate through his belief in reincarnation, according to Buddhism, and his misinterpretation of that belief. Personally, I believe in reincarnation, but it's not what I hope for. The goal is to get the hell out of this world, and suicide isn't the way.

Jumbo bribed the Vice-Commander, and moved back a few days later. For Kong's funeral, he prepared a table with joss sticks, fresh fruit and duck. The Chinese prayed with joss sticks between their palms. Kong's clothes, pictures and other property were burned piece by piece. This was to sever any bond to the world.

Steven Harris was also a Buddhist. He was a junkie from England and had been injecting a lot of heroin. He knew that the jones was a nightmare compounded upon his nightmare. Two weeks after Kong's death, Steven went to his cell half an hour early. He wrote a farewell letter to his mother, shot his last gram of heroin, and then hung himself.

He was found hanging in his cell, three cells from mine. His deep-blue face was frozen in a panic-stricken gaze. The key-boy quickly locked his cell. He was left hanging until the British Embassy arrived four hours later. The Embassy couldn't understand how two of their nationals could commit suicide within two weeks. When the autopsies revealed high levels of heroin, they questioned whether it was suicide or murder.

I knew the kitchen would be cooking. I warned Jumbo, but it was too late. It became impossible to quit. The Garden was flooded with heroin and everyone was strung-out. The Chinese competed to sell it. Credit was given liberally just to sell it. The Building Thief didn't care. He got his envelopes.

Under the guise of an important meeting with the Vice-Commander, the Blue-shirts and Commodores called all of the foreigners into the Thai chow hall. Once inside, they swiftly padlocked the gate behind us. Unfazed, the foreigners sat on benches drooling and nodding.

Troops of new Commodores marched in double-lined. Taking up the rear, a shaggy-haired drug dog, doped up and tail wagging, trotted in with his tongue hanging-out sideways. Everyone broke in laughter. We couldn't tell who was higher, the dog or us. Several hours later, they came out empty-handed. Everyone thought it was over.

Within a week, every Commodore in the section was removed, including the Building Thief. A new sheriff was in town. A surprise raid was sprung at 8:00 a.m. Dozens of Commodores and Blue-shirts swarmed into the Garden. Everyone was still in their lockers getting a morning fix. Five Chinese got nailed with heroin. They were interrogated in the cellblock. This was their first meeting with the new Building Chief, now called the BC. The Chinese were beaten in the cellblock and put in chains. They squealed their guts. They were then locked into a new Soi called the Black hole.

The Black hole was the last ten cells on the second floor, at the end of the 'T' cellblock. The cells were dirty, paint-peeling holes. The bars of the steel door were blocked with plywood. None of them had fans. Sectioned off from the main population, access was restricted.

The BC was in his early thirties, medium height and physically fit. He was from a wealthy family and un-bribable. Prior to this, he worked at Bangkwang Prison. He knew the game well. Heroin was brought in by the kilos there. His job was to clean up Section two. To let us know what was happening, the BC walked through the Garden and announced the new rules. "Medicine, ma be lai (no problem with pills), but if you caught helloin, no chance," he said, serious.

The BC prepared a hit list. Suspects were taken into the cellblock for interrogation. Those who didn't have an embassy were beaten mercilessly. He knew they couldn't complain. The black hole filled up. Suspects who had an embassy were moved to Section five, including Jumbo.

The BC entered a different hut everyday with his new squad of Commodores. The huts were torn apart and trashed. The cells were also torn apart. All shelves and bookcases were thrown out. A lot of money was found. No heroin. Nobody was exempt, including Ollie. His superiority complex finally got him in trouble.

"You're small and powerless as a bug," Ollie told one of the BC's Commodores. Ollie was immediately moved to Section five.

The BC was skilled in Martial Arts and kickboxing. He strutted around in khaki's tucked into his black combat boots. Thais cringed when he passed. The foreigners hated him. To show-off his talent, he did a spin-kick to the face of a Burmese refugee. We weren't impressed. He blew it when he beat two Chinese that he thought were from Red China. They were from families that lived in Hong Kong and America. They filed formal complaints with the American and British Embassy. The embassies contacted the Director of the Thai Corrections Department. The American Embassy investigated the situation. We wanted the BC removed.

The British Embassy promised appropriate action. It became a political power struggle.

The BC tried to compromise with the Chinese. He promised to leave them alone if they dropped their complaint. They didn't want to hear it. "I'll match power for power," the BC threatened. The Chinese didn't buck. In retaliation, their huts were torn apart and they were moved into dirty cells.

An order came down from the Commander of the prison. The BC would be moved to Section five. The BC became friendly all of a sudden. He called a meeting and told us the news. He also told us that we would be moved with him. I didn't believe him. I knew how manipulators think.

Tempers flared. The ooga-booga's were non-stop. The Paki's cried to Allah, "Mother F...ers want to kill us."

"What are we going to do?" everybody asked. I said it was a bluff. "But what if it isn't?"

A lot of money had been invested in the Garden over the years, and everybody was broke from the heroin binge. We couldn't afford to build new houses in another section, so the Garden went on a hunger strike.

The BC helped us write a petition, written in Thai. "We want to stay in Section two and keep the Building Chief with us," it translated to say. As a compromise, we promised to quit using heroin if he stopped his rampage. A week later, the order to remove the BC was rescinded. I had no regrets. Ollie was moved out of the hut, and the heroin circus stopped. Satisfied that he completed his task, the BC changed his stance. He played soccer and Takraw with the prisoners, and no longer caned the Thais.

CHAPTER TWELVE

DESTINY

"How's the Bitch, Hollywood?" I asked, our code name for the female pot plant growing on the roof, inside of the Bougainville bush.

"Righteous, I just got done watering her," he said.

"Yeah, I can tell," I said, chuckling. "It looks like it's raining with the water pouring off the roof. Do you think anyone will catch on?" I asked.

"Nah, nobody would ever think we were crazy enough to grow ganja, especially with the BC's rampage," he said.

"Yeah, but what do you think would happen if the BC caught us?" I asked.

"Why? Ganja is organic. It's not heroin. The BC doesn't care what we do, as long as we don't use heroin," Hollywood said.

"Yeah, I guess you're right," I said, "And he's pretty cool now-a-days. Everyone seems to be healthier and happier too."

After five months, our Bitch was ripe and ready to harvest. To celebrate Clinton's Presidential victory, we harvested on Election Day, November 4, 1992. Yes, we did inhale. Waterbed and Captain Krunch transferred home a month earlier. They had served five years, and became the fourth and fifth Americans to be transferred on the treaty. This was the second round of transfers, two and a half years after the first. We questioned how long it would be until the next.

Shortly afterwards, Ollie's pardon was denied. He finally requested to transfer home on the treaty. I'd be eligible to transfer the following year, and Hollywood would be eligible to re-apply in a few months. I assumed that we would all go home together. Ollie wasn't thrilled with the thought.

Hollywood and I shared the American hut with three cats. Momma cat, known as Slut-Bitch Psycho, was a mesh of orange, black and white. She was totally out of her mind, and perpetually pregnant. Every few months she'd dump a batch of kittens, sometimes at my feet, and then abandon them. The rats devoured them. Her only surviving babies were Cat-man and Shit-head.

Cat-man was orange and white, and smart as a dog. He was the biggest cat in the Garden. A tough old cat that everybody loved, he had scratches across his face, bitten ears, and chunks of hair missing. Nightly battles produced new wounds that didn't have time to heal. He limped into the hut every morning, crawled into a lounge chair as if he owned it, and slept the day off.

Shit-head was a stunted, kitten-sized female Calico. She just ate, slept and never left the hut. She became my pet kitty. I fed her leftover fish-heads and bones. On cold mornings, she would crawl into my lap. Shit-head didn't understand what happened when she got pregnant. When it was time to give birth, she literally ripped them out of her stomach. Her first batch of runts resembled Cat-man. Within a few days, her unattended litter was eaten by the rats. Psycho got pregnant faster than she could abort. Shit-head in turn stole Psycho's litter, and then abandoned them. The rats got another round of kitty delicacies.

November 19, 1992 was my thirty-sixth birthday. I had one year left according to Mr. Kamul. Convinced that it was my last birthday, I threw a party. We devoured six large pizzas, two apple pies, and two kilos of Tiger prawns. The following week, we were called out to the Vice-Commander's office.

The Consulate and Judy Dominguez, our representative, surprised us for Thanksgiving. The pokerfaced Consulate was dressed in a three-piece suit. Judy had a clean white dress with ruffles. Ollie was in his crisp Boy Scout attire. Hollywood and I wore ragged shorts and old blue shirts. They brought turkey, mashed potatoes, cranberries, pumpkin pie and all the stuffings.

Hollywood mimicked a Woody Woodpecker laugh. I stuttered like Porky Pig. Ollie stood at attention with his mouth open in awe. As we stared at the feast, I couldn't help wonder if it was too good to be true. Questions swirled in my head as I read the looks on everyone's faces. *What's the catch? Are these the same people who've been chucking us off all these years? Is this the last supper, or have they suddenly had a change of heart?*

"Thanks a lot, we really do appreciate it," I said. "What's for Christmas?" I asked, as we sat down.

"Would anybody like to say grace?" the Consulate asked.

We looked at each other with the "Who us?" look.

"Rub a dub-dub, thanks for the grub. Praise God," Hollywood and I blurted out simultaneously, and then chuckled at the irony of our timing.

It was a rare treat, but I got used to being hungry. Hunger pains were a part of life. The Hong Kong Triad raised guinea pigs. Jumbo referred to them as "Hairy rats." They barbecued the hairy rats when they grew large enough. I thought it was pure savagery, until I got hungry. A plate of fried guinea pig on rice wasn't the tastiest dish, nor do I plan to eat it again, but it was better than other dishes consumed.

By New Years of 1993, the heroin problem was a distant memory. Everybody looked and felt better. As a reward, the BC set up tug-o-war contests and bag relays. A live band played in the chow hall. Katois were brought in as dancing girls. Gambling was blatant. Pictures were taken everywhere. It was rare to have pictures, and the first time a camera was allowed in the Garden. I posed in the water trough shower and in my garden. I looked like a scrawny POW in a concentration camp. Everything was going right as we headed into the New Year. It felt as though I was on a roll again.

The Europeans organized a New Years backgammon tournament. It started as a friendly winner-takes-all event. Ten of us anteed a carton of cigarettes. I won the ten cartons. The Austrians couldn't accept the fact that I won. They had played in professional tournaments and were obsessed with the game. I was a rookie. Determined to beat my lucky streak, this one-time tournament turned into a daily ritual. They played a very strategic game. However, I was a rare breed that they couldn't come to grips with.

"That's a stupid move," they scoffed whenever I made an irrational move. Yet I still won. I called the desired numbers before rolling the dice, and they'd roll out on command.

"No more calling the dice," they demanded, frustrated.

"What do you mean, 'No calling the dice?' What do you think? I'm talking to the dice? Do the dice have ears? C'mon, you can talk to the dice too," I teased.

"But it's impossible. Nobody would ever do that in a tournament," they cried.

"I agree with you a hundred percent, I'll be the first to admit that I don't know how to play this stupid game. I'm just the luckiest f...er in the world," I said.

It wasn't a fluke. I knew they'd never win. It was the same scenario as when I played it in Oahu Prison. I told them to quit. This made the challenge greater. Every morning for two weeks, three Europeans lined up and waited their turn. It was strictly cash on the table. We played sets of two out of three, for twenty dollars a set. I won five hundred dollars, and quit when they became poor losers. Unfortunately, we became adversaries after that, and I didn't play backgammon ever again.

I firmly believe in spiritual laws that defy physical laws. Greed is a syndrome that goes against spiritual laws. Generosity opens the regulator that allows it to flow. From my perspective, greed caused them to lose. It's complicated to understand, and as unexplainable as the power of prayer. Yet, life is full of things that are mysterious, including Dan's return to Thailand.

Dan was freed within a year of his extradition to Florida, and visited us from the other side of the fence. I smelled a rat. Friends to the end are just friends until they get caught. Dan lured Hollywood with promises of instant riches. Visions of grandeur sparked his desperate financial situation. Hollywood approached every drug trafficker with a deal. In turn, I warned everyone. He even asked me to arrange a million dollar heroin deal.

"Yeah sure, I can give him a map to Burma," I said, to brush him off. After being set-up, I knew that I wasn't being paranoid. To cover my back, I immediately wrote to Phil Lowenthal, my attorney in Hawaii.

Ollie's application to transfer was approved. Hollywood re-applied. Ollie wanted to leave immediately. We all did. He expected them to come and get him when he wanted to go, as if it was his right, and pressed Judy Dominguez at every chance. He failed to realize that they transferred prisoners in groups, and only two groups of prisoners had transferred. Nobody else would be eligible for a few years. I was eligible to transfer in July of 1993, four months away. I didn't want to miss the boat, so I asked Judy to process my application.

"I'm sorry, you can't apply until you've served four years," she said, feigning sincerity.

"What do you mean? The treaty says we're eligible to transfer after four years. Not eligible to apply," I said.

"I'm sorry, that's what I was told," she said.

"Well if you're not going to process my transfer application, will you support my Medical Pardon?" I asked humbly.

"Medical Pardon?" Judy asked, suddenly straightening up, "You have a Medical Pardon?"

"Yeah sure," I said casually, "I filed it over a year ago, and Doctor Jon recommended it," I bluffed. She had filled numerous prescriptions for me, so she had no reason to doubt it. I can imagine her discussion with the DEA afterwards.

Judy returned the following week, and informed me of their sudden change of heart. I was elated, but Ollie was visibly disappointed. There was a lot of bureaucratic red tape involved in transferring. I had to be approved by both governments. After I was approved and eligible, they had to arrange the transfer. It would entail bringing an attorney and Federal judge to Thailand. They also had to make arrangements to transport us to Los Angeles. The Bureau of Prisons (BOP) would pick us up, and they needed at least one man per prisoner. Finally, they had to coordinate a time when everybody could meet in Thailand.

My transfer was approved a few months later. Hollywood was denied again. I assumed that his involvement with Dan sabotaged his transfer. A week later, a bag of ganja was found in the pocket of a shirt hanging on the clothesline of our hut. A Thai squealed on me. We had a good rapport with the BC by this time, but he couldn't show favoritism. I was chained and sent to the black hole.

It was hot season. The cell door was blocked with plywood. A breeze was rare if ever. The only air came through a two by two-foot barred cell window that faced the AIDS Garden. A toxic odor of raw sewage rose from the Garden. The humidity and stench created a cesspool-type sauna. I sat in my underwear and sweated profusely. It was too hot to sleep during the day.

The black hole was breeding grounds for sewer rats. They scurried from cell to cell scavenging. Huge, slimy sewer rats crawled into my cell through the squat toilet. They were fat, some as big as small cats. I felt a rat run over me when I was sleeping. To escape, it squirmed under the door. To keep them out, I blocked the squat toilet with a large Pepsi bottle. My rubber slippers covered the space under the door. This kept the rats at bay until I had to use the toilet. The head of a rat popped up while I was taking a pee once. If I was squatting, it could've bitten my ass. I cringed at the thought.

The hole in OP was no comparison to the Black hole. The scenario was identical though. I was almost out of prison when I was sent to the hole for smoking a joint. Now I was in the Black hole for a bag of weed. Pot wasn't worth it anymore. I thought a lot. I wondered if I had changed my destiny. Ganja wasn't as serious as heroin, but I could get an inside case. This would prevent my transfer.

After three weeks in the rat-infested hole, the BC granted an amnesty on his birthday. Within hours of my release, the Nigerians created a scene over something trivial. This caused a conflict between the African and Thai prisoners. A riot almost broke out between them. The BC was tired of the drama, especially on his Birthday, so he supported the Thais.

The Nigerians wrote another petition to remove the BC. Nobody supported them. My only concern was to live in peace and harmony. I wrote a petition to remove the Africans out of the section. Not all of them, just the ones who didn't want to live together peacefully. I made a lot of enemies. They took it as an infringement of their rights, as if they had any. In the end, the BC was removed from Section two.

When the BC left, two Nigerians confronted me in the American hut. One of them was Kendrick. He was from the first group of Nigerians to move into the Garden. He had always been a problem. I saw the play before they walked in. I grabbed a butcher knife and hid it under the pillow of my chair.

"Hey Andy, we want to talk to you a minute," Kendrick said, when they came into the hut.

"Sure, come in, have a seat," I said calmly. I sat on the chair where my knife was stashed. They sat across from me. "What's on your minds?" I asked.

"We've been waiting a long time for this," Kendrick said. Just then, Hollywood walked in.

"Hey guys, what's up," he asked, not realizing that a confrontation was taking place.

"Oh nothing," I said nonchalantly. "Have a seat. We're just having a talk," I said, as I kept direct eye contact with the Nigerian across from me.

Hollywood sat in the chair to my right. Kendrick was across to my left. The vibes were tense. The dialogue was unfriendly. Suddenly, the Nigerian stood up and tweaked my nose to intimidate me. I thought he was making a move. I pulled out the butcher knife and lunged at him. Hollywood grabbed my arm within inches of his throat. The African was stunned. I was furious. After heated words between us, they backed off.

After that, Kendrick extorted other foreigners. He threatened to tell on them if they didn't pay him a bribe. He returned and tried to take my Walkman. I was told to "give it up by Monday or else." That was the last straw. Through a Thai Kayai, I paid to have him hit on Sunday. Sunday was the Thai's free day. Thirty Thais surrounded Kendrick when he went to the Thai-side of the section. Sticks, stones, bricks and lockers crashed down on him.

He immediately snitched off the Thai who threw the first stone. The Thai was moved to another section. Kendrick was put into chains and the black hole. He stayed there for several months. It was a perfect arrangement. Afterwards, Hollywood and I held a meeting in the American hut with a few of the Brotha's.

"So what do you guys want to do?" I asked Mike, one of the leaders. "We're all prisoners here. Do you want to live together or do we have to fight all the time?"

"No man. Everything's cool. We just want to be friends again," Mike said. The Nigerians didn't like Kendrick either. He was an embarrassment to their race. We called a truce, shook hands and smoked a joint.

The world weighed heavily on me by this time. At times I didn't think I'd get out alive. My application to transfer was finally approved and processed. I was anxious to leave, but the Embassy wouldn't tell us when we'd go. "Soon," was all they would say. Soon to them could be forever.

Three older misfits arrived, a German, Brit and an Australian. The Brit looked like a gravedigger with his wide stained teeth and sinister smile. We named him the Gravedigger. The German walked as if he was on a ship in high seas. He rocked back and forth, and grasped anything reachable for support. He had an equilibrium problem. The Australian seemed to be the only one with any hope. He was sixty-years old, had curly white locks, and seemed to be in top shape physically.

"Hey Andy," Hollywood said, pointing to the Australian in chains. "I think I know that guy from somewhere."

"Yeah, me too," I said, as I searched my memory. "I know!

That's King Neptune, King of the seven seas."

"Yeah, you're right," Hollywood laughed, "He looks just like him, especially with the Capricorn tattoo on his arm."

I moved King Neptune into my cell. King Neptune grew up in Yugoslavia, now Bosnia, but had Australian citizenship. I didn't ask how he was able to change his citizenship. I just assumed it was political. He was very intelligent and knowledgeable, and had some unusual stories that came across as factual. I wondered if they were all true. He was an arms dealer who got caught up with the gravedigger. They had three kilos of heroin. He swore that he was innocent and was fighting his case.

King Neptune professed to be a Muslim turned Christian. He came up with a scheme to sell the Muslims a phony nuke bomb. Under the guise of being a fellow Muslim, he planned to sell them a nuke for a million dollars. He may have had the connections, and seemed to have the caliber to pull it off. I didn't give it much thought at the time though. Years later I did. King Neptune was acquitted and released after five years; a miracle in itself. A few years later, Al Qaeda claimed to have a nuke.

King Neptune was a recent convert to Christianity. I told him that I was a Born-again Christian. He didn't understand what it meant to be Born-again. I wasn't the best example. My sister brought my Bible when she visited, but it sat on the shelf. It finally hit me when the train arrived for the thousandth time. After the whistle blew, I heard a rooster crow. Roosters crowed every morning, but the analogy didn't register until then. I identified with Peter when he denied Christ the third time and a rooster crowed. It was the wake-up call. I started to read my Bible again.

The Nigerians held a service in the cellblock every Sunday. A Christian congregation now flourished. My appearance amazed the Brotha's one Sunday morning. Nobody knew that I believed. Life was hard for them, so I gave a short sermon on suffering. "Our present sufferings aren't worth comparing with the glory that will be revealed to us," I read from Romans 8:18.

A month prior to my transfer, the large purple orchid that I divided into four separate pots all bloomed simultaneously. I was thrilled. It was the first time that they bloomed in three years. I would've been happy if just one flower bloomed. Instead, two to three large, purple, sweet fragrant flowers blossomed from each pot. It was a blessing that I took as a sign. I knew that I was going home.

On November 4, 1993, two weeks before my thirty-seventh birthday, I was called out to the Vice-Commander's office. Ollie was already there. We met the attorney who would represent us at our transfer treaty hearing. The hearing was being held at the Immigration Detention Center in Bangkok. They told us that we'd leave the following day.

The following morning, the Thais and American Embassy held a news conference at the front office. It was a historical moment. I felt like a POW leaving Vietnam. They posed and shook hands. Movie cameras rolled and cameras flashed. I became the sixth American to be transferred out of Thailand on the treaty. It was hard to believe that we actually left Klong Prem. Taken to Immigrations in the back of a Toyota truck; we zipped down the freeway that was non-existent in 1989.

The Thai Immigration Center was a human zoo. Over a

hundred and fifty prisoners, from over thirty countries, were crammed into a space of fifteen by twenty-five feet. We slept in shifts. Half of the room sat up for twelve hours. The other half slept. As a last fling, I bought a joint. I vowed to quit using drugs when I left Klong Prem. It wasn't fun anymore. I seriously prayed for sobriety, and quit on the spot.

A Federal Judge and Public Defender from North Carolina completed the formalities. The procedures were as if entering a guilty plea in court. It included signing away our rights to an appeal.

"I don't think they'll be able to wipe the smile off their faces until Christmas," the Judge remarked afterwards.

"You kidding?" I said, "We've had these smiles on our faces since last Christmas."

"Is that when the Embassy told you that you were going?" he asked.

"No, that's when my Chinese astrologer told me," I quipped, as if in jest.

The Judge roared in laughter. "Well, I guess that's about all you can bank on in this country," he said.

"You can say that again," I said with a wide smile, knowing I would've been committed to a nut ward if he knew that I was serious.

We were transferred out of the country within fourteen hours. The Warden from Los Angeles Detention Center (LAMDC) picked us up at 5:00 a.m., with three deputies from the Bureau of Prisons. We were taken to Don Muang Airport, and caught the 8:00 a.m. flight to Los Angeles, via Hong Kong.

In route to Hong Kong, we flew over Laos and Vietnam. We had a spectacular view of the Golden Triangle and the brown-watered Mekong River. I was in deep thought as I reflected on my nefarious adventures throughout South-east Asia. I'm not sure if I felt like I was going home or had left home, but it was a chapter I intended to close. I didn't look back.

EPILOGUE

L AMDC seemed like a hotel. I hadn't used a telephone in five years, and the thin prison mattress was the softest bed that I had slept on in years. Having a full stomach was a new high. We were fed three meals a day for free. My attention zeroed in on the box of toilet paper that was given out liberally. I instantly saw dollar signs as I calculated its value. *Twenty-five cents, times two hundred rolls, that's fifty bucks worth of crap paper*, I thought to myself.

I thought that I was in top shape when I left Thailand, but immediately I noticed how big everybody else was. I weighed 120 pounds. With my mustache, dark tan and scrawny figure, I was mistaken for a wetback. Even the Mexicans were fooled.

We were given a complete physical. My teeth were cavity infested. I needed a few root canals and numerous crowns. They noted the scars on my ankles from the chains, and I was diagnosed with post-traumatic stress disorder (PTSD).

Ollie and I became buddies. The transfer was a bonding experience. He went back and forth to court in San Francisco, and his subsequent charge of exporting twenty-five tons of Marijuana was worked out. He was released on parole. I also met Jerry while in LAMDC. Jerry was a co-defendant of Dan's in the Marco Polo gang. Jerry had been on the run for six years. He was the last gang member to be apprehended. Like Dan, he was charged under the RICO Act. His discovery revealed that Dan had in fact co-operated.

In preparation for the parole board, I received documentation concerning my indictment. It revealed the status of my co-defendants. Kastner's eight-year sentence was cut in half after he testified in front of the Grand Jury in the kilo case. Brent, the financier in that case, was given two and a half years for his extensive co-operation with the government. Wayne, my business associate, was sentenced to five years. They were all out of prison by this time. The District Attorney in Hawaii dropped the charges against me, but forwarded the information to the parole board. It was used as "Relevant conduct" in calculating my guidelines.

Relevant conduct is a vague rule that can include anything deemed to be related to the offense. This meant that my guidelines would include the kilo of heroin in the Kastner case, even though I wasn't tried or convicted for that offense. Using this information, the probation officer calculated my guidelines at fifteen years. As a treaty case, my only hope for a departure banked on the harsh conditions. It was a departure based on "Unusual circumstances not taken into consideration by the Sentencing Commission when formulating the guidelines."

The parole board took my circumstances into consideration. They also noted that the sentencing guidelines were established for equalized sentencing. "It wouldn't be fair to get fifteen years when the co-defendants got less than five." They re-calculated my guidelines to seven years. The five years served in Thailand were credited towards my sentence. I was also given fifty-four days off per year for good time according to US law.

After six months in LAMDC, I was transferred to Florence FCI in Colorado. It was a huge and modern facility; Disneyland to me. I served another year there, until released to a Federal halfway house in Hawaii for the last six months of my sentence.

The halfway house was an essential transition stage for me. I was broke and starting my life over. I worked two jobs, returned to surfing, and found a Christian church within walking distance of the halfway house. I was thirty-eight years old and ready to settle down. To keep me on the right track, I needed a nice girl who didn't use drugs. The pretty Japanese girls visiting Hawaii infatuated me. They seemed to be genuine, down to earth and drug free. I prayed for a beautiful Japanese girl who could speak English. For extra measures, I prayed for one whose birthday coincided with mine. The birthday part of my prayer wasn't vital; it was an afterthought. I thought it would be cool, because it was a special bond that my mother and I shared.

The day before my release from the halfway house, I ate dinner at the Makai Marketplace food court at Ala Moana shopping center. I bought a Chinese plate dinner, and then looked around for a vacant table. In the midst of the crowd, I saw a beautiful, classy Japanese girl, sitting by herself.

"May I sit here, please?" I asked her.

"Yes, please do," she said. Her name was Kumiko. She was eating Japanese food. We talked and ate. Kumiko was polite and stunning. I laid on the charm. We had a pleasant conversation, and eventually talked about our ages and birthdays. Kumiko was thirty-four years old. I was thirty-eight. The age difference was perfect. When she told me that her birthday was November 21st, two days after mine, I looked up to the heavens and chuckled. *You gotta be kidding*, I said to myself. This time I took it as a sign. I drove her home and she gave me her phone number.

The following day, I checked out of the halfway house. I called her five minutes later, and took her out to lunch. A few days later, I took her to my friend's twentieth class reunion. We sat in the banquet room at Nicholas Nicholas, one of the finest restaurants in Honolulu. A romance followed and we married the following year.

A few days before our marriage ceremony, our families met for the first time. We had cocktails at the Kahala Mandarin hotel, on the lower terrace near the ocean. The sky was clear as we watched the sunset past Diamond Head. A trio of Hawaiian musicians serenaded us as we exchanged gifts. When they started to play the Hawaiian Wedding Song, a remarkably light misty rain swirled in the air. The mist was comfortable. Considered a Hawaiian blessing, it continued throughout the entire song. Near the end, it turned into a light drizzle. I thought it was going to rain. The song finished and the drizzle immediately stopped on cue. It was perfectly timed, from beginning to end. The musicians were in awe.

"Wow, Spoooky," the guitarist said wide-eyed, looking to his left and right.

"Yeah, chicken skin, brah," the ukulele player said, scratching his arms.

Here we go again, I thought, as I smiled and looked up to the Heavens.

COMMENTARY

The United States incarcerates more people per capita than any other country in the world. Does that mean that America has the worst people on Earth? The State of Hawaii spends over 50 million dollars a year to ship prisoners out of state to privately owned prisons. The result is a prison problem with no solution, a methamphetamine epidemic that leads the nation, and a homeless population never seen before. Statistics show that eighty percent of those incarcerated have drug or alcohol problems. Should they be punished, or treated? In the past, there was a balance between rehabilitation and punishment. However, the pendulum swung towards punishment in the 1980s, and got stuck. Over twenty-five years of punishment mentality and the only solution is three-strikes you're out?

On the road to recovery, the average addict relapses three times. Three relapses are three-strikes for many addicts. I'm coined a "three-time loser," but I refuse to buy the program. "Three-strikes you're out" is a cheap way for society to get off the hook for its failures. If we convince people to believe that they're losers, then we create losers. A baseball coach doesn't teach his players to strike-out; he encourages them to hit homeruns. Everybody remembers Babe Ruth for his homeruns. A little known fact is that he holds the record for the most strike-outs. It's the same with drug addicts or anybody for that matter. When they have incentives, encouragement, and opportunities, they hit homeruns.

"Love thy neighbor" and "Pray for your enemies" aren't just wise Biblical sayings. It's what life is about. I believe that we've lost focus on the reason to incarcerate. Prisons have a purpose, but long term incarceration should be reserved for violent criminals. Unfortunately, all convicted felons are stereotyped as violent rapists and murderers, yet most are non-violent drug addicts.

Drug addiction isn't criminal; it's social. Most addicts commit crimes to feed their habit—crimes that stop when they become sober. Drug addicts are stuck in a cycle of delusion. Similar to temporary insanity, there is simply no logic to their actions. They'll do anything to get drugs. Once you're hooked, it's next to impossible to stop. "Once an addict, always an addict," isn't a cliché, it's a fact. The mind is a computer. All habits are programs permanently stored in the memory. All it takes is a taste, and the habit is recalled. "Just once won't hurt," is a rationalization that triggers the recall button. Once leads to twice, and then they're hooked again. It's similar to a cigarette smoker who quits smoking for ten years. All it takes is one cigarette, and they're hooked again.

Sobriety is a lifelong course. However, new programs can be created to substitute habits. When we re-program our thoughts, we change our habits. It's a long process, but in due time, anything can be turned around.